T0316593

# Cambridge Elements ≡

Elements in Construction Grammar
edited by
Thomas Hoffmann
*Catholic University of Eichstätt-Ingolstadt*
Alexander Bergs
*Osnabrück University*

# CAN CONSTRUCTION GRAMMAR BE PROVEN WRONG?

Bert Cappelle
*University of Lille and CNRS, UMR 8163 STL*

CAMBRIDGE
UNIVERSITY PRESS

Shaftesbury Road, Cambridge CB2 8EA, United Kingdom

One Liberty Plaza, 20th Floor, New York, NY 10006, USA

477 Williamstown Road, Port Melbourne, VIC 3207, Australia

314–321, 3rd Floor, Plot 3, Splendor Forum, Jasola District Centre, New Delhi – 110025, India

103 Penang Road, #05–06/07, Visioncrest Commercial, Singapore 238467

Cambridge University Press is part of Cambridge University Press & Assessment, a department of the University of Cambridge.

We share the University's mission to contribute to society through the pursuit of education, learning and research at the highest international levels of excellence.

www.cambridge.org
Information on this title: www.cambridge.org/9781009478786

DOI: 10.1017/9781009343213

First published 2024

*A catalogue record for this publication is available from the British Library.*

ISBN 978-1-009-47878-6 Hardback
ISBN 978-1-009-34320-6 Paperback
ISSN 2753-2674 (online)
ISSN 2753-2666 (print)

# Can Construction Grammar Be Proven Wrong?

Elements in Construction Grammar

DOI: 10.1017/9781009343213
First published online: January 2024

Bert Cappelle
*University of Lille and CNRS, UMR 8163 STL*

**Author for correspondence:** Bert Cappelle, bert.cappelle@univ-lille.fr

**Abstract:** Construction grammar has gained prominence in linguistics, owing its popularity to its inclusive approach that considers language units of varying sizes and generality as potential constructions – mentally stored form-function units. This Element serves as a cautionary note against complacency and dogmatism. It emphasizes the enduring importance of falsifiability as a criterion for scientific hypotheses and theories. Can every postulated construction, in principle, be empirically demonstrated not to exist? As a case study, the author examines the schematic English transitive verb-particle construction, which defies experimental verification. He argues that we can still reject its nonexistence using sound linguistic reasoning. But beyond individual constructions, what could be a crucial test for Construction Grammar itself, one that would falsify it as a theory? In making a proposal for such a test, designed to prove that speakers also exhibit pure-form knowledge, this Element contributes to ongoing discussions about Construction Grammar's theoretical foundations.

**Keywords:** falsifiability, Construction Grammar, cognitive linguistics, syntax, verb-particle constructions

ISBNs: 9781009478786 (HB), 9781009343206 (PB), 9781009343213 (OC)
ISSNs: 2753-2674 (online), 2753-2666 (print)

# Contents

# 1 Introduction: The Stakes

"Religion gives us certainty, stability, peace. It gives us absoluteness which we so long for. It protects us against that progress which we all dread almost more than anything else.

Science is the very opposite of that. Science is always wrong and science never solves a problem without raising ten more problems."

(George Bernard Shaw in a speech honoring Albert Einstein, transcribed in the *Manchester Guardian*, 1930)

Construction Grammar, as proposed by influential linguists like Fillmore, Kay, and Goldberg, is one of today's prominent linguistic theories (Hoffmann & Trousdale, 2013; Nikiforidou et al., to appear). The present installment in a series on Construction Grammar (CxG) delves into the critical examination of whether this theory can rightfully claim a place as a scientific one. My specific objective in this Element is to address the fundamental question: Is CxG a falsifiable theoretical approach?

## 1.1 Beliefs Held Dear by Most Construction Grammarians

As a framework, CxG is adopted in numerous empirical research papers that report testable findings. Undoubtedly, much, perhaps most, of what is published under the banner of CxG contributes to the corpus of sound scientific knowledge. Yet, for all the quantitative observations it helps us to formulate, CxG is often reduced, as a theory, to a few almost inspirational quotes. Construction grammarians (CxGians) hold certain core beliefs, many of which are unshakable. They rally behind assertions like "it's constructions all the way down," and the certainty that "constructions are cognitively real."

The former claim is an oft-quoted aphorism by Goldberg (2003: 223), the latter a statement that almost 80 percent of 189 CxGians who participated in a recent survey (Boas, Leino, & Lyngfelt, to appear a) agree with. Most respondents to this survey also *dis*agree with the statement that "[t]here are constructions without meaning" – not surprisingly, when constructions are standardly defined as "pairings of form and meaning," or "form-function units."

Yet, there remains limited exploration and testing of these and other foundational ideas. Instead, they are presented as "axioms," "basic ideas," "convictions," "postulates," "premises," or "principles," as if they were non-provable themselves and are simply needed to get the actual linguistic work off the ground.

One such relatively unchallenged and untested idea is the proposition that no principled division exists between small constructions, equivalent to single words, and larger ones, spanning phrases or sentences. All these units, whatever their size, are said to have meaning. Furthermore, most CxGians argue that the distinction between concrete constructions, with lexical material already in place, and abstract ones, comprising open slots for lexical content, is arbitrary. These claims allude to there being a "continuum" between lexicon and syntax or between words and rules.

This Element raises the question of whether these fundamental tenets have undergone thorough empirical scrutiny, and if such an endeavor is even sought after within the CxG community. Construction Grammar, as it stands, may appear to be more a collection of unchallengeable assumptions than a system of refutable conjectures.

In the pages that follow, we will embark on a journey to explore the testability of constructions and of CxG. For the former, a single abstract construction, which has been claimed to be unfalsifiable by someone from the inner circle of CxG itself, will serve as a test case. As for CxG itself as a linguistic theory, we will take aim at some of the repeated grand claims it makes, and especially at the contention that all the structural knowledge that speakers possess about a language is linked with meaning.

## 1.2 Popping the Falsifiability Question

The question addressed in this Element is the one that Thomas Hoffmann (2022: 281–284) asks at the end of his recent textbook on CxG: "Is Construction Grammar a falsifiable theory?" Hoffmann here touches on an important issue, raised also in a squib by him, whose main title was likewise in question form: "What would it take for us to abandon Construction Grammar?" (Hoffmann, 2020). It might seem odd that Hoffmann, a prominent figure in CxG, who helped elevate the theory to the canon of linguistic research, for instance by virtue of the CxG handbook he coedited (Hoffmann & Troudale, 2013), should take an interest in counterevidence against what CxG proposes, counterevidence strong enough to jettison the whole theory. Is Hoffmann being perverse, one might wonder, in trying to find ways of undermining the theory so dear to him and others? Wouldn't it be more fruitful to ask how CxG can be buttressed so that it doesn't risk crumbling down?

By raising the question of CxG's falsifiability, Hoffmann really does act in the best interest of the theory. He wants us to reflect not just on whether CxG makes linguistically correct claims but also, more crucially, on how the whole constructionist enterprise can survive as a scientific undertaking. In this Element, I will address Hoffmann's question against the background of its proper wider context, which is Karl Popper's (2002[1959[1934]]) philosophy of science. According to Popper, formulating clear hypotheses and putting them up for testing – and consequently, if need be, allowing them to be refuted – is what demarcates a scientific enterprise from non- or pseudoscientific goings-on.

We have seen that CxG, in addition to being a theory, is also, or perhaps in the first place, a framework within which researchers carry on their work as CxGians. Some of that work is known as "constructicography" (e.g., Lyngfelt et al. 2018), which involves the identification of recurrent lexicogrammatical patterns in a language. These together make up the "constructi-con" – the network of constructions assumed to represent speakers' linguistic cognition (Diessel, 2023). Keen linguists, often with the help of computer scripts that trawl corpora in search of combinations of words and/or parts of speech with an unexpectedly high frequency, may perceive a pattern in language and therefore posit a "construction." However, just because a linguist can detect a pattern, this doesn't necessarily mean that the human mind belonging to an individual speaker also "sees" this pattern.

Remember that most CxGians do believe, though, that constructions don't just emerge as regularities emerging from corpora but also reside in the mind. Is there any way of knowing whether the "constructions" that we as linguists postulate are indeed cognitively real? This is the sort of question that has plagued cognitively oriented linguists for quite some time (e.g., Sandra & Rice, 1995; Divjak, 2015). And precisely this concern was recently voiced again by Hoffmann (2020): On which grounds can CxGians simply go about making the claim, as they tend to do, that this or that construction does or does not exist in the constructi-con, and therefore in cognition?

Hoffmann mentioned the example of two different views within CxG – one of them being my own – which seemingly make opposite claims about the existence of a particular candidate construction, the transitive verb-particle pattern with variable word order (e.g., *send {in} the FBI {in}*). On one view, there is a schematic construction that doesn't specify the word order of the particle vis-à-vis the direct object noun phrase (NP). On another view, there are just two specific word orders which are directly linked to one another as sisters, obviating the need for a schematic "mother" construction.

It might appear outrageous to suggest that an entire linguistic theory would have to stand or fall by its ability to determine whether a single proposed construction should be recognized as one. Still, this specific case is symptomatic of a general problem and will therefore be given quite some attention in this short monograph.

## 1.3 Which Brand of Construction Grammar Is Focused on Here?

There are many versions of CxG (see Butler & Gonzálvez-García, 2014: 80–112, for a useful overview, and see Ungerer & Hartmann, 2023, for recent contextualization of CxG as one of the "constructionist" approaches). It is therefore necessary to clarify the specific variant or "flavor" at the core of this work. The version I'm focusing on is "cognitive CxG" or "usage-based CxG," sometimes also referred to as "Goldbergian CxG." This is probably the most popular variety and because it has laid out its theoretical assumptions clearly it is also well known outside the CxG community.

Usage-based/cognitive CxG makes the claim not only that constructions serve as useful tools to describe acceptable linguistic expressions within a language but also that these constructions are acquired through exposure and, hence, possess cognitive reality. As Hilpert (2021: 4–5) writes, CxG constitutes "a theory of what speakers know when they know a language, that is, when they know how to produce and process language." We saw in Section 1.1, however, that most but not *all* CxGians share the belief that constructions are cognitively real. Those who adopt varieties that put a heavy emphasis on representational formalization or computational implementation may not be concerned that much with whether or not the constructions that they identify and represent are also mental categories. These CxGians would then also not hold the claim that constructions are cognitively real so strongly, or at all.

Figure 1 provides an overview of the main principles of cognitive/usage-based CxG. In this figure, I have taken the liberty to add in the first tenet (left) the crucial information that the pairings of form and function should be either unpredictable or sufficiently frequent (or both) to count as constructions. Furthermore, I have replaced the formulation of the second tenet (still left) as it appears in Goldberg's (2003: 219) list ("An emphasis is placed on subtle aspects of the way we conceive of events and states of affairs") with the more telling first sentence of the section in which she explains this principle. Goldberg (2003) discusses under that section the well-known constructionist principle that phrase- or clause-level constructions, such as the ditransitive construction ([verb someone something]) or the caused-motion construction ([verb something/someone somewhere]), carry meaning by themselves, as well as the correlate that different syntactic constructions differ in meaning or function.

As the lines in the figure indicate, a single tenet can sometimes be unpacked as several specific ideas. Note, for instance, that Goldberg's (2003) first tenet, about the essential similarity of units at all levels of linguistic analysis, can be shown to have correlates with five separate formulations in Hilpert's (2021) overview. Conversely, the first, third, and seventh of her tenets are summarily captured by his idea that "[a]ll of linguistic knowledge is a network of form-meaning pairs – constructions – and nothing else in addition" (Hilpert, 2021: 6). This latter part seems important, and I will treat it that way.

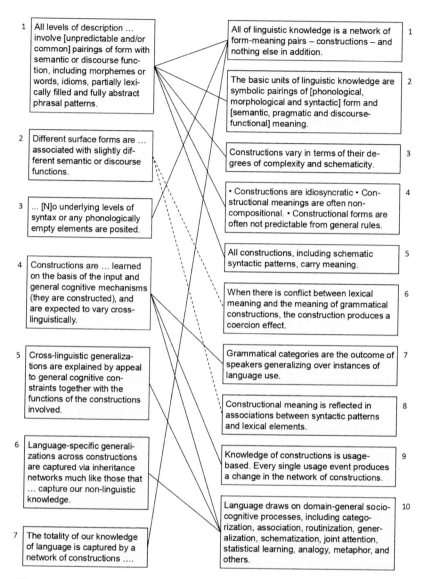

**Figure 1** Constructionist "tenets" or "basic ideas" of CxG, as formulated in Goldberg (2003; left) and Hilpert (2021; right). Full lines indicate obvious correspondences between the claims and dotted lines more indirect ones.

Two comments are in order about equating *Goldbergian* with "usage-based" and with "cognitive," as was done earlier. Firstly, it's noteworthy that Goldberg explicitly adopted a usage-based perspective in her work only with the publication of her 2003 manifesto-like paper. In this important paper, she expanded upon her well-known earlier definition of constructions as form-function units, as outlined in

Goldberg (1995: 4). Notably, this revised perspective encompassed all units that exhibit sufficient frequency of use, even if they are formally and functionally unremarkable. To illustrate this point, consider the phrase *I apologize for the inconvenience*. On Goldberg's original definition (Goldberg, 1995), this wouldn't qualify as a construction due to its absence of idiosyncrasies or non-compositionality. However, under the updated definition, its high token frequency is reason enough for its classification as a construction. This is because its frequent occurrence suggests that speakers of English, or at least a portion of them, have memorized this sequence as a whole.

Secondly, proponents of cognitive CxG may not universally endorse all of Goldberg's ideas, particularly her earlier ones. For instance, Hans Boas argues that specific grammatical behavior associated with verb classes and even individual verbs – which he refers to as "mini-constructions" (Boas, 2003, 2008) – deserves as much attention as the broad argument-structure constructions that Goldberg (1995) famously focused on. While the concept of *Goldbergian* constructions typically evokes general constructions such as the ditransitive and the resultative construction, as well as other highly abstract and schematic structures with meaning, Goldberg's more recent research acknowledges low-level, item-specific aspects of constructional knowledge as having as much importance. This emphasis on the specific is not incompatible with appreciating the general. Goldberg contends that the most general grammatical patterns allow us to describe scenes that humans are familiar with from infancy, such as handing something to someone, altering the location of an object, moving our bodies from one place to another, and so forth. She has termed this concept the "scene-encoding hypothesis" (Goldberg, 1995: 39). Consistent with this overarching idea – that our grammars facilitate communication about our shared human experiences – is to also recognize specific constructions that are conventionally used to describe more concrete actions falling under the broader categories of transfer, caused motion, and similar general scenes.

In any case, focusing on a variety of CxG that assumes that constructions have a counterpart in the mind, or even the brain, has its implications for our discussion, which can then center on the following questions, specifically:

- Are posited constructions-as-mental-units always subject to falsification?
- Can we test the claim that the *entirety* of our language knowledge consists of constructions, understood as pairings of form and function?

## 1.4 Looking Ahead

This section offers a glimpse of the organizational structure for the remainder of this Element. In Section 2, I will examine sociological and psychological factors that can give rise to unhealthy dogmatism within CxG and lead to complacency among its practitioners. In Section 3, I will explore the concept of falsifiability within the framework of Popperian philosophy of science. Despite debates about the importance of falsifiability, I defend its relevance in theory construction. In Section 4, I will discuss in some detail the postulated construction that Hoffmann (2020) argued could not be falsified. I will suggest that it can, by using a kind of *reductio ad absurdum* argument, as more empirical methods are not available. I will then, in Section 5, move on to the issue of whether CxG as a comprehensive theory, not just one of the many posited constructions, is falsifiable. I consider three auxiliary hypotheses, the syntax-lexicon continuum, isomorphism, and the domain-generality of linguistic knowledge, before attempting to formulate a crucial test for CxG's core idea that our knowledge of language can *exhaustively* be described as form-function units. Section 6 concludes with the hopeful message that, while the theory may not be 100 per cent correct in some of its central claims, its "bold conjecture," as Popper would term it – namely, that what we know about language are meaningful constructions – stimulates us to think about the function of forms in a vigorous way that we might not without this conjecture.

## 2 Can't Touch This: Does Construction Grammar Have an Attitude Problem?

[B]y far the greatest danger in scholarship (and perhaps especially in linguistics) is not that the individual may fail to master the thought of a school but that a school may succeed in mastering the thought of the individual.

(Sampson, 1980: 10)

In this section, I provide some discussion of the circumstances in which linguists do their research, as I believe getting insight into the historical, sociological, and maybe even psychological aspects of science are relevant to a critical assessment of CxG. This theory is enjoying a momentum of popularity. At the same time, and precisely because researchers feel they have the wind at their back, there is little serious discussion anymore of its foundations. Construction Grammar being one of the functional-cognitive approaches, its principles used to be formulated in direct opposition to generative-linguistic orthodoxy, but the younger generations, it seems to me, are no longer that interested in the old debates, so that there is little fresh deliberation of opposing views. Functionalists and cognitivists have long discredited generative linguists' belief that there is an innate, cognitively encapsulated grammar module. Nevertheless, I will argue that it may be good to keep an open mind to findings from the neurosciences that suggest that the wholesale rejection of a specialized language faculty is not justified.

## 2.1 Being on a Roll

Today, CxG stands as one of the primary options for those seeking a well-established theory of language structure. How many alternative theories are there around? Certainly not as many as James McCawley's (1982) book *Thirty Million Theories of Grammar* suggested in its title – this was an outrageous number even around the time it was published, in the heydays of theory formation and proliferation when "a veritable alphabet soup of competing frameworks [came] into being" (Newmeyer, 1996: 156; cf. Harris, 2021: 269–285). There still are several theoretical options to choose from (Müller, 2023), but CxG, especially when it first appeared on the scene, presented itself as the main rival to one approach in particular, that of "mainstream" generative linguistics developed by Chomsky and his followers.

Müller (2018: 1), indeed, sees the contemporary theoretical-linguistic land-scape as bipolar: "Currently, there are two big camps in grammatical theory: the Chomskyan research tradition (Chomsky, 1981, 1995) going back to earlier work by Chomsky (1957) and the more recent framework of Construction Grammar (CxG, Fillmore, Kay & O'Connor, 1988; Goldberg, 1995, 2006; Tomasello, 2003)." Can we trust the accuracy of Müller's appraisal? We probably can, given that he pledges full allegiance to neither camp: "I believe that I can make such a statement since I am working in a minority framework myself (Head-Driven Phrase Structure Grammar)" (Müller, 2018: 1, fn. 1). But more to the point, he gauges the relative popularity of theories based on such factors as the number of dedicated journals and conferences.

Considering just the CxG side, the series within which the present Element is published appears alongside an older and still-running one, Constructional Approaches to Language (published by John Benjamins), established in 2004 and boasting at the time of writing a catalog of more than thirty volumes. Apart from these two book series, there are two journals devoted to CxG: the open-access journal *Constructions*, which started in 2004, which is all set up for "entering a new era" (Hartmann & Sommerer, 2022), and the Benjamins-published journal *Constructions and Frames*, which first appeared in 2009, and publishes two issues a year. The latter journal also caters to CxG's sister theory, frame semantics, whose origins go back to work by Charles Fillmore (1982, 1985a), one of the founders of CxG (see Fillmore, 2020, for an anthology of his seminal and later texts on CxG; see Boas, 2021, for a presentation of both theories). There are, furthermore, two handbooks of CxG, one published by Oxford University Press (Hoffmann & Trousdale, 2013) and another by Cambridge University Press (Nikiforidou et al., to appear), as well as two introductory textbooks applied to English (Hilpert, 2014; Hoffmann, 2022).

There is a biannual conference spanning up to five days, with six or more parallel sessions. Smaller-scale workshops on CxG are organized more frequently than that, giving CxGians the opportunity to regularly meet up and share their newest analyses, methods, and insights. There is, in short, no denying that CxG is going strong.

As in so many domains of society, polarization is a process that, once set in motion, seems to resist all efforts of being countered. Respective adherents of the opposing theories are driven further away from each other as the common ground between them gets smaller. Third options become marginalized and forgotten about, their practitioners getting vastly outnumbered by proponents of the two main remaining theories. If there is a psychological or sociological explanation for this, it likely includes, among other factors, some sort of FOMO – fear of missing out. For instance, many scientists tend to go to large festival-like, recurring conferences where all the action is, the big names perform, and collective memories get constructed, rather than attend fringe events around niche topics that are allowed to be tackled in theoretically diverse ways but where, speaking from personal experience, it may be hard to follow presentations that are couched in a theoretical framework different from one's own. The only hope of survival for independent theories appears to be to give up their full independence and align with either of the two major movements. This allows them to be classified and tolerated as one of the many "dialects" of one of these main theories.

Around the beginning of the twentieth century, it was still possible to write that "construction grammar has emerged as an important trend in cognitive linguistics" (Taylor, 2003: 225). Nowadays, the label "trend" does little justice to CxG, which has become something of a norm, if not *the* norm. As a term printed in published books, "construction grammar" has overtaken, or is outpacing, several alternative theories (both competing and more allied ones), as can be seen in Figure 2.

Construction Grammar also comes out on top if it is compared with a set of different search terms, such as "biolinguistics" (after government and binding theory and the minimalist program, the most recent incarnation of Chomsky's linguistic approach), "role and reference grammar," "dependency grammar" and even the very generic "functional grammar" (with or without capitals). Construction Grammar clearly can no longer be perceived as waiting in the wings, poised to take on the stage. It has firmly established itself as a lead actor.

As pointed out, in the early days of CxG, its proponents felt compelled to stake out its territory and lay down its principles, typically in direct opposition to the then-reigning Chomskyan approach, which detached "Core Grammar" from "The Periphery" as well as syntax from semantics, grammar from lexicon, and competence from performance (see, e.g., Fillmore, 1985b, 1989, on these and other

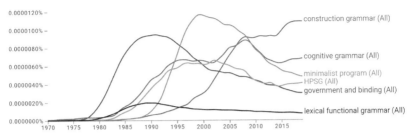

**Figure 2** The waxing and waning of linguistic theories, via Google Books Ngram Viewer. The Y-axis shows the frequency with which the search terms appears in the corpus of Google Books in a particular year, from 1970 to 2019 (the most recent year for which the search could be done). Searches were case-insensitive, so all capitalization variants of a name are shown as a single trend line.

"familiar dichotomies" to be rejected as false). The major differences between CxG and "mainstream" generative linguistics are still occasionally repeated in conference presentations, science papers and monographs that brand themselves as taking a "constructional," "constructionist," "construction-based," or indeed a "Construction Grammar" approach. However, CxG has become such a widely adopted and broadly applied theory that it has itself become mainstream and that such assertions about being different are no longer necessary. I suspect that many master-level and even doctoral students currently find themselves adopting a constructional perspective to a particular phenomenon long before getting wind, if at all, of the existence of a radically different approach to their topic of study or without being in the slightest concerned with what an alternative approach might have to say about it. There can be excuses for what I make out here as ignorance or deliberate oversight, as when the phenomenon one deals with poses such descriptive challenges that even just getting the facts right, using some corpus-based or other empirical methodology, is a sufficiently worthwhile endeavor, obviating the need to present any analysis from a theoretically different vantage point. And often, there simply *is* no known alternative.

CxG presents in many respects such a simple and elegant view of language that one can hardly be against it. In CxG, as we have seen, there is no strict dividing line between syntax and lexicon as there were in some major earlier linguistic theories. Almost anything is therefore eligible to receiving the status of construction, from absolutely normal combinations to idiosyncratic quirks of language, from highly abstract structures to concrete word sequences, and from small schemas specifying how to use a mere morpheme to conventional ways of structuring entire discourse structures – think of cooking recipes. This might give researchers the warm, fuzzy feeling that they cannot possibly be wrong in calling a phenomenon of interest a construction.

Not only does CxG, by virtue of its similar treatment of words and larger structures, have the allure of a beautiful, unified theory, it may also strike one as so reasonable in its assumptions that one may be left wondering how one could ever *not* be a CxGian. As "construction," which CxG gives again due attention to, is a traditional notion, often used synonymously with "structure," we can see the theory as a continuation of much pre- and non-Chomskyan thinking about grammar. Precursors and contemporary allies can be found in various places on the Old Continent. See, for instance, Bouveret and Legallois (2012: 8–13) on constructionist perspectives in French linguistics.[1]

CxG is likely to attract many new followers for years to come. Its future success looks all the more assured because it has proved to be combinable with new ideas without losing its essence. Over the years, we have seen the emergence of various areas of constructionist research, such as:

- diachronic CxG (among many others, Noël, 2007; Barðdal, 2011; Traugott & Trousdale, 2013; Sommerer & Smirnova, 2020; Hilpert, 2021; Noël and Colleman, 2021), where constructionist ideas are brought to bear on questions of language change;
- pedagogical or applied CxG (Holme, 2010; De Knop & Gilquin, 2016; Boas, 2022), which recognizes that language teaching should be all about constructions ("what else?" as Herbst (2016) remarks);
- diasystematic CxG (Höder, 2012, 2019; Hendrikx & Van Goethem, 2018), which is interested in the representation of both language-specific and unspecific constructions in the linguistic competence of bilingual or multilectal speakers.

These are just some of the extensions of CxG to particular domains of inquiry.

## 2.2 Dangers

Construction Grammar has thus become a mainstream, reasonable-looking, low-threshold, open, malleable and apparently future-proof theory. Yet, some dangers are looming. These can be summed up as follows:

- Labeling something as a construction seems risk-free; yet, we're unsure if speakers have corresponding mental representations.
- "Construction" is in keeping with other theories, potentially blurring CxG's distinct identity.

---

[1] I have known a now-retired colleague in France who proclaimed he was a CxGian *avant la lettre*, as he had been carrying out CxG-style research long before the framework reached France from the States. Conversely, there are also linguists holding out against CxG, or so they say, but whom we, constructionists, know to be closeted CxGians and who may need some time to discover that constructionism is their true theoretical identity.

- Construction grammar's popularity may lead to dogmatism and complacency among its proponents.
- There's a potential danger of overlooking findings that challenge established CxG principles.

I will elaborate further on each of these dangers, which, as will become evident, are interconnected.

First, subscribing to a constructionist framework is taking relatively few risks. With the expansion of Goldberg's (1995) definition of constructions to frequent combinations (Goldberg, 2003/2006), phraseological units are also considered constructions. The term *construction* itself is not technical and has been used, and continues to be used, in "traditional" grammar, as noted.[2] Furthermore, it seems almost impossible to write an article on syntax without using the word *construction*, even if one does not work within this theory or even ignores its existence. Outside of CxG, *construction* is often used to refer to the outcome of some syntactic process – in other words, it is used for something that in CxG circles would be called a *construct*. The fact that the metalanguage of CxG relies on such a common term can support an "(almost-)everything-is-a-construction" viewpoint. However, calling something a construction carries with it the implication that speakers have some sort of mental representation of whatever is branded a construction. That is because in (cognitive/usage-based) CxG, constructions are claimed to be mentally stored clusters of information that generalize over individually encountered instances of language use. But do we always have evidence for that?

Second, the concept of construction, in the sense of Goldberg (2003/2006), is compatible with other theories, which means that CxG is not fully unique in its claims. For example, CxG aligns with pattern grammar (Hunston & Francis, 2000), not surprisingly, but also, to various extents, with role and reference grammar (Van Valin & La Polla, 1997; for discussion of the concept of construction in this theory, and the theory's compatibility with CxG, see Nolan and Diedrichsen, 2013), systemic functional grammar (Halliday & Matthiessen, 2013), word grammar (Hudson 2006; for discussion, see Gisborne, 2011) and cognitive grammar (Langacker, 1987). All these approaches assert that they are in harmony with the idea of construction. In the case of Langacker's cognitive grammar, the author goes as far as to claim that the theory he developed in the early nineteen-eighties, initially called space grammar, was, in essence, an early version of CxG, before the term existed: "Although the term had not yet been invented, the theory I formulated was actually a kind of Construction Grammar" (Langacker, 2005a: 102).

---

[2] See, however, Haspelmath (2023: 3) for an interesting note on the history of the word *construction*, whose use as a count noun (as opposed to its use as a mass noun, synonymous to *syntax*) is more recent than many a CxGian presumably thinks it to be.

Goldberg (2006: 220–225) concurs that cognitive grammar and CxG share numerous tenets but highlights some points of disagreement with Langacker's comparison of the two theories. Langacker (2009), in turn, provides reasons for having "certain disagreements about this list of disagreements" (Langacker, 2009: 168), concluding that "Goldberg overstates the differences" (Langacker, 2009: 167). This is a prime illustration of what was expressed in Section 2.1, specifically that the sole prospect for independent theories to live on seems to involve relinquishing their complete autonomy and affiliating with a more dominant theory. This seems to have worked for cognitive grammar. However, this comes with the danger that the unique theoretical contributions of these affiliating theories may get overlooked – cognitive grammar, for instance, uses specific terms and concepts that not all CxGians would use. But there is also the risk for CxG to suffer genericide: by fragmenting into too many different varieties, it could see its own identity diluted.

Third, there is the double risk of dogmatism and complacency. Given the highly sectarian state of theoretical linguistics, many CxGians hardly ever get to mingle with hardcore generativists, who hold rather different beliefs about language and who many CxGians feel it is fruitless to attempt to persuade to see things differently. And if CxGians move almost exclusively within a milieu of CxG-friendly colleagues, repeating the basic principles of the theory, however summarily, can be expected to be met with nothing but approval. This is the classic echo chamber situation.

*Not* repeating the principles explicitly is also a valid option, as one doesn't need to state the obvious or preach to the converted. Because there are more interesting matters to attend to – doing actual constructionist research – and because CxG is so well established that it doesn't need much justification anymore, I have the impression that the central principles of CxG are less and less laid out, let alone discussed at length. If the research that is carried out squarely fits into the constructionist framework, the findings will have the effect of providing implicit confirmation of what its adherents are already convinced of. Moreover, there is safety in numbers: if so many linguists do CxG research, they can't all be wrong, can they?

The result of all this is that principles on which CxG are founded can lead an unhindered life. As the popular saying goes, if all you have is a hammer, everything looks like a nail. Translated to CxG: if the concept of a form-function pairing is the only legitimate theoretical concept, form-function pairings are all we have eyes for. Any formal property of language that lacks a clear semantic correlate may thus be overlooked and, likewise, any semantic or pragmatic mechanism without discernable, stable morpho-syntactic substance may remain outside the scope of CxG research (see Leclercq, 2023, who for that reason argues for making a bridge with relevance theory).

Fourth, and obviously related to the previously mentioned twin problem, many CxGians may not be fully aware of findings from neighboring fields that call into question something believed to be beyond dispute, namely the idea that when we process sentences, we just work with general-purpose cognitive mechanisms. This may turn out to be not really the case. Construction Grammar has inscribed itself in an even more general school of linguistics, namely cognitive linguistics (for introductions, see Evans & Green, 2002; Geeraarts & Cuyckens, 2007; Dąbrowska & Divjak, 2015; Ungerer & Schmid, 2006; Dancygier, 2021; Xu & Taylor, 2021), which means that it strongly opposes viewpoints central to its main rival, generative linguistics. While generative linguistics seems to be flawed in many respects – worst of all, perhaps, it seems to have become no longer falsifiable (see, e.g., Woschitz, 2020: 155, and Section 5) – it may be right about one thing: humans have a *special* knack for language; that is, their linguistic skills are of a different kind than any other cognitive skills. This will be discussed in some detail in Section 5.2.1.

Everything (or almost) a construction, everyone (or almost) a CxGian, entrenched ideas, self-satisfaction, some myopia – these are by far not the only dangers that CxG faces. For instance, Boas, Leino, and Lyngfelt (to appear) point out that, since CxG itself provides a cornucopia of different flavors, there are many, often incompatible, ways in which constructional insights are being represented in a metalanguage or formalization. Practitioners of one variety of CxG therefore struggle to see how the terminological machinery and notational conventions used by those of another variety are compatible with their own representational habits. Construction grammarians who prefer to keep formalization light might wonder whether some of the more technical formalisms aren't beside the point of making a theoretical observation, while those who insist on some degree of rigor may be exasperated by colleagues who appear to eschew notational precision.[3] What we see is that within an echo chamber there are – if the imagery doesn't break down here – various echo corners.

## 3 Falsificationism: A Still-Influential Approach to Scientific Inquiry

Science at its best is a public, testable, challengeable project, always having to maintain its own respectability by saying what would serve as counter-evidence against its hypotheses and concepts.

(A. C. Grayling, in Edmonds and Warburton, 2010: 233)

---

[3] It is sometimes assumed that couching an analysis in a rigid formalism is a way of making the claims more precise, testable, and hence falsifiable (e.g., Sag, 2012: 70). I beg to differ. See Tallman (2021) for some discussion, specifically of why a formal analysis fitting phenomena in one particular language does not contain falsifiable hypotheses for another.

The idea of falsifiability as a criterion for scientific belief systems goes back to work by the philosopher of science Karl Popper (2002[1959[1934]], 1963). Popper advanced falsifiability as a crucial property for science, by which it can be distinguished from pseudo- or non-science. Only if a belief system is propped up by propositions that, in the light of empirical observations, could be proven false can it be considered scientific. This section looks at this proposed criterion, asking whether or not we should adhere to it at all times. While I will be dealing here with concepts and distinctions of a general philosophical or metascientific nature, I will illustrate them, where possible, with examples from linguistic research.

### 3.1 Propositions and Theories in the Balance: Popper's Falsificationism

Popper holds that theories are only falsifiable insofar as they make concrete, testable predictions. When claims are so vague that they can't be subjected to testing, they cannot be falsified and hence cannot be recognized as being scientific. An entire belief system that can only be characterized by vague, untestable (and hence unfalsifiable) claims is, accordingly, not scientific either. Astrology is an oft-cited case in point. Falsifiability is Popper's demarcation criterion for science: it is by this property that sciences can be distinguished from other, non-scientific belief systems, such as pseudo-science or religion.

Hoffmann (2022) refers to Popperian philosophy of science when he points out that "[o]ne of the hallmarks of scientific theories is their falsifiability; that is, the fact that they make predictions that can objectively be proven wrong . . . . So, can we actually falsify Construction Grammar? Is it a proper scientific theory?" (Hoffmann, 2022: 281). In this passage, Hoffmann raises the falsifiability issue about two related but, I would argue, far from identical objects: propositions (i.e., claims, predictions) and theories (which allow us to formulate certain propositions and whose credibility depends on the perceived correctness of those propositions). In practice, falsifiability is typically applied to both these ontological entities and sometimes it is impossible to tease apart propositions from theories, especially when a theory can be captured as a single proposition – as in the case of, for instance, the flat Earth theory, which proclaims quite simply: "The Earth is flat." For our discussion of a more complex theory such as CxG, though, it is best to identify two distinct questions of falsifiability.

In the one case, the question is whether concrete claims made by CxGians are testable. The answer to this can be answered in the positive for certain CxG-generated claims. For instance, the cognitive relatedness of specific posited constructions, such as the passive construction (e.g., *The 747 was radioed by the airport's control tower*) and the locative construction with another preposition than *by* (e.g., *The 747 has landed near the airport's control tower*) can be, and has been, tested empirically. This has been done in a psychological priming experiment, where one tests how easily a string is recognized after a rapidly presented stimulus (e.g., Branigan et al., 1995). As it happens, the two constructions turn out not to be related (Ziegler et al., 2019).

Being able to falsify the entire theory, however, is a different matter altogether. What is at issue here are the very foundations of the theory, including such general assumptions as the view that there is nothing about language knowledge that cannot be modeled as form-function units, the view that lexicon and syntax form a continuum, the view that what we utter and hear is never the output of any transformational processes on underlying semantico-structural representations, and so forth. What hangs in the balance here is not just the correctness of a specific claim – in the example given, a claim of the type "construction A is (not) related to construction B and therefore A will (not) prime B" – but the correctness of the entire theory. It will be clear that this issue is the more vital one.

The falsifiability questions are not unrelated in this specific example, which exemplifies in a more subtle way the point illustrated by the flat Earth theory/proposition. When Ziegler and colleagues (2019) tested whether locative constructions not containing a prepositional phrase (PP) with *by* can prime passives with a *by*-PP, this was meant to be a stress test for a foundational claim by which CxG profiles itself as a theory among alternatives, namely that language users do not store in their construct-i-con any syntactic templates without substance or meaning (i.e., mere "tree diagrams"); if they did, these would serve as primes for constructions that happen to have the same phrase structure configuration. The apparently rather particular finding here supports the correctness of the theory.

Supporting the correctness of a theory may be possible, but *proving* its correctness is beyond reach. Popper's falsificationism differs starkly from inductivism, an alternative approach to scientific inquiry which assumes that a theory can be proven true by accumulating more and more evidence in its favor. Indeed, his falsification principle entails that we can merely *corroborate* a theory. That is, we can only accept the soundness of a theory provisionally, for the time being, without ever being able to confirm it definitely. Instead, Popper argues, we can *disprove* it definitively. The famous example given by him is that of the "theory" – actually more a proposition – that all swans are white (Popper 2002[1959[1934]]: 4). Finding ever more exemplars of white swans will never do to prove that the theory is right, but observing a single black swan will forever have proven it wrong. This, then, is how science should work for Popper: not trying to continually support theories and their hypotheses but attempting to disprove them once and for all. Only by subjecting scientific theories and the propositions they generate to rigorous experimentation and by looking for evidence that would falsify them can we find out their strength. If our theories and hypotheses can withstand the falsifying tests, they are considered to be strong, if not necessarily indefinitely correct, while those that are falsified by experimental evidence are rejected. They then have to be modified, at the very least, or replaced with better ones.

## 3.2 Relaxing Strict Falsificationism

Popper's falsificationism is very strict. It requires the researcher to specify *in advance* under which empirical circumstances the proposition or theory must be given up: "real support can be obtained only from observations undertaken as tests (by 'attempted refutations'); and for this purpose criteria of refutation have to be laid down beforehand: it must be agreed which observable situations, if actually observed, mean that the theory is refuted" (Popper, 1963: 38, fn. 3).

This strict procedure is sometimes unrealistic. For one thing, just because certain claims (or "tenets") do not come with an immediate instruction of how to test them does not mean that they hold no scientific value. Researchers could advance them as valuable insights, leaving it to others, perhaps scientists of later generations, to find ways of operationalizing them as predictions.

The philosopher Imre Lakatos, a prominent disciple of Popper's, rejected as idealistic and untenable what he called "dogmatic falsificationism," that is, the logic by which "science grows by repeated overthrow of theories with the help of hard facts" (Lakatos, 1970: 97; emphasis removed). Dogmatic falsificationism leads to a caricature, whereby "the history of science is seen as a series of duels between theory and experiment, duels in which only experiments can score decisive victories" (Lakatos, 1974: 311). Believing that the falsification principle alone is responsible for progress in science, he argued, would mean that much of our everyday research activities are to be seen as irrational and unscientific. In any case, entire theories are not discarded whenever the smallest observation turns up that runs counter to what could have been predicted.

In practice, scientific theories are not refuted that easily – certainly not large-scale, well-established ones like CxG, which is what Lakatos (1974: 316) might call a high-end "system of theories," given that it does not make one single theoretical claim but includes various theoretical assumptions (cf. Section 1.3), each of which is almost a theory in its own right. Applying Popper's falsificationism to such a supra-theory would hardly have the (for Popper) desirable effect of refuting it when a part of that theory turns out false, as it would "[allow] the imaginative scientist to save his pet theory by suitable lucky alterations in some odd corner of the theoretical maze" (Lakatos, 1974: 317). Or as Salkie (1984: 204) puts it: "there is no reliable way of telling which part of a theory a falsification falsifies, and … any theoretical idea can be maintained at some price."

Moreover, scientists generally just learn to live with problematic facts, inconsistencies, apparent or real paradoxes, criticism from inside or outside the community, and so on:

> [I]n large research programmes there are always known anomalies: normally the researcher puts them aside and follows the positive heuristic of the programme. In general he rivets his attention on the positive heuristic rather than on the distracting anomalies, and hopes that the "recalcitrant instances" will be turned into confirming instances as the programme progresses. … This methodological attitude of treating as *anomalies* what Popper would regard as *counter examples* is commonly accepted by the best scientists. Some of the research programmes now held in highest esteem by the scientific community progressed in an ocean of anomalies. (Lakatos, 1974: 317)

Each sufficiently mature research program has what Lakatos (1970) calls a tenacious "hard core," which is difficult to attack directly, as scientists active in that program use their "ingenuity to articulate or even invent 'auxiliary hypotheses,' which form a protective belt around this core. … It is this protective belt of auxiliary hypotheses which has to bear the brunt of tests and get adjusted and re-adjusted, or even completely replaced, to defend the thus-hardened core" (Lakatos, 1970: 133).

An example from linguistics that immediately comes to mind is the universal grammar (UG) hypothesis in generative-linguistic theory. Chomsky himself would probably agree with this: he calls the ability of children to learn language thanks to their specifically linguistic genetic endowment "the core theory of language – Universal Grammar" (Chomsky, 2005: 4). The idea that there is such a thing as UG has remained central and sacred in Chomsky's research program. Criticism of it is deflected to specific auxiliary hypotheses, such as the argument from the poverty of the stimulus (Chomsky, 1965), the competence/performance distinction (again Chomsky, 1965) and various concrete proposals about the underlying structure of all languages, such as the A-over-A constraint (Chomsky, 1964) or X-bar theory (Jackendoff, 1977). These supporting assumptions have been attacked, adapted or superseded by alternative proposals, leaving UG itself scot-free, at least in the eyes of practitioners of this research program.[4]

---

[4] For critical discussion of the argument from the poverty of the stimulus, see, among others, Pullum and Scholz (2002), Clark and Lappin (2011), and Sampson (2016). The competence/performance distinction is forcefully and unanimously rejected by scholars working within cognitive linguistics, which emphasizes the importance of studying language in use, in context, and as an integrated aspect of human cognition and communication. As Evans and Green (2002: 110) put it: "In rejecting the distinction between competence and performance cognitive linguists argue that … knowledge of language is knowledge of how language is used." Comprehensive criticisms of the UG hypothesis are offered by Evans and Levinson (2009a, b) and Dąbrowska (2015).

Popper's ideas have come under further criticism. Feyerabend (1975), for instance, argued against the notion that there is a single, universal scientific method that all scientific inquiry should adhere to. Feyerabend contended that scientific progress is not solely based on a fixed set of rules, like Popper's principle of falsifiability, but is characterized by a rich diversity of methods, approaches, and historical contingencies. Thomas Kuhn is perhaps the most famous critic of the strong emphasis Popper places on the role of a so-called "crucial test" that would falsify an entire theory if it produced an observation counter to prediction.[5] In periods of what Kuhn (2012[1962]) calls "normal science," researchers are not devoted to attacking bold conjectures in order to sink a theory; rather, they get to work with the theory as it is, staying within the paradigm. Using an example that the reader will be familiar with, Goldberg's (2006) book *Constructions at Work* could be seen as "paradigmatic" in Kuhn's sense, that is, exemplary of standard construction-based research activity, providing a model to large numbers of "normal" constructionists who get inspiration from the scientific breakthroughs it presents.

In times of normal science, researchers jointly try to spell out the key facts and findings of a theory, highlight the hypotheses that provide better explanations for problematic facts than competing theories do, and bring to light new data to add to an ever-growing stock of facts. Kuhn speaks of three types of research problems which we can see being addressed in research journals in non-revolutionary times: "determination of significant fact, matching of facts with theory, and articulation of theory" (Kuhn, 2012[1962], 34).

Speaking more generally, normal scientists engage in "puzzle-solving activity," that is, they address problems that are considered relevant within the reigning paradigm. The puzzles to be solved are not necessarily anomalies that scientists attempt to explain away. In Kuhn's philosophy, the puzzles that are solved in times of normal science tend to be relatively easy problems with standard ways of solving them: "like someone doing a crossword puzzle or a chess problem or a jigsaw, the puzzle-solver expects to have a reasonable chance of solving the puzzle, that his doing so will depend mainly on his own ability, and that the puzzle itself and its methods of solution will have a high degree of familiarity" (Bird, 2018). In CxG, such a puzzle might be, for example, the mildly intriguing observation that in English you can say *prefer*

---

[5] A full survey of criticisms of Popper in the philosophy of science is beyond the scope of this work (not to mention my expertise). Note, though, that some more contemporary philosophers of science advocate for Bayesian approaches that consider the likelihood of theories being true or false rather than relying solely on rigid falsifiability criteria (e.g., Williamson, 2017; Sprenger & Hartmann, 2019). Yet other approaches adopt insights from formal learning theory (e.g., Kelly, 1996).

*to do something* but also *prefer doing something*; a solution to this puzzle might consist in finding other lemmas that exhibit this alternation and running a collostructional analysis (Gries & Stefanowitsch, 2004) to find out which of these lemmas tend to occur with which particular complement verbs in which alternative, and so get a grip on possible subtle meaning differences between the alternatives, in line with basic idea #8 on the right side of Figure 1 (Section 1.3).

In Popper's eyes, a single reproducible anomaly can and should topple a theory. Not so for Kuhn, who argues that in day-to-day scientific research, anomalies are typically ignored, until they are getting too numerous and troublesome to keep sweeping under the rug. In times of normal, non-paradigm-shifting science, falsification is only used with an eye to developing and refining the theory where needed. Normal scientists are conservative tinkerers, not revolutionists.

### 3.3 Falsifiability as an Ideal

In spite of such criticism, Popper's views on the role of bold hypotheses and falsification are still widely influential among researchers across scientific disciplines (Riesch, 2008). In recent years, we have even seen something of a Popperian revival. Derksen (2019) describes how in scientific fields that suffer from difficulties to see experimental results confirmed, specifically in social psychology (Earp & Trafimow, 2015), reformers are promoting new ways of publishing research that are very much in the spirit of Popper's ideas.

One new publication type is the registered report (RR). Here, a researcher submits a comprehensive study proposal to a journal, which includes a detailed outline of their data collection and analysis methods. Expert reviewers evaluate the proposal based on criteria such as the significance of the research question and the quality of the research plan. If the proposal meets the necessary criteria and is accepted, the final research report is assured publication, irrespective of the actual study outcomes, as long as the research plan has been faithfully executed. The RR procedure offers the dual advantage of preregistration (whereby researchers craft a comprehensive data collection and analysis plan, which receives an official timestamp when they upload it to a repository) and the commitment to publishing findings, even if they yield negative results. This approach significantly enhances the likelihood of theories being subject to potential falsification, as all outcomes will be published, even null results, which can in some cases prove wrong a hypothesis or theory (namely, when that hypothesis or theory would predict a significance difference).[6] Clearly,

---

[6] Although null hypothesis significance testing is in line with Popper's falsificationism (e.g., Wilkinson, 2013), it has been the topic of some debate, especially because it can be blindly applied and even be used in manipulative statistical practices aimed merely at achieving desired results (so-called *p*-hacking). In quantitative linguistics, Sönning and Werner (2021) have recently

carefully specifying *in advance* what one aims to test – and, crucially also, what the outcome of the test would mean for the theory (Meehl, 1990; Scheel et al., 2021) – is in line with Popper's strict guidelines.

It is fair to say that, whether knowingly or unknowingly, Popper's falsification principle is almost universally adopted as a guideline in science, forming part of the standard definition of science, even if it is just an *ideal* of what science should be like. As Lakatos (1974, 312) writes, "Popper's definition of science can best be put in terms of 'conventions' or 'rules' governing the '*game of science.*'" It's true that academics don't always "play science" so strictly by the rules as Popper has laid them out, with the statement of a falsifiable hypothesis as an opening move and either tentative corroboration or inexorable rejection of the hypothesis or theory as the goal of the game. Yet, researchers do recognize that what matters for the scientific status of a theory is their willingness to abandon it in the face of sufficient and sufficiently strong counterevidence. They also realize that there should be some consensus on the kind of evidence that would be needed to prove the theory wrong.

With CxG fully matured, we should by now have reached some agreement on what would count as really damning counterevidence. The point Hoffmann (2020, 2022) makes is that we don't seem to know precisely what would constitute the kind of findings that would prove that CxG is irredeemably flawed. Assuming that critical tests do have their role to play in scientific progress, what *are* the crucial experiments to be conducted to try and prove CxG wrong? In the light of Popper's demarcation criterion of science, Hoffmann's question is meant to make us reflect on this, even though, as we have seen here, abandoning CxG will never be as easy as parting from the belief that all swans are white on a single sighting of a black one.

## 4 The Particular but Generalizable Problem Posed by Particle Verbs

> There are, however, a large number of productive subcon[s]tructions of *V* that deserve some mention, since they bring to light some basic points in a rather clear way. Consider first such verb + particle (*V* + *Prt*) constructions as "bring in," "call up," "drive away."
>
> (Chomsky, 1957: 75)

Particle verbs, also commonly known as "phrasal verbs," have long fascinated syntacticians. If they are words, how can they be split up? But if they are

---

argued for a Kuhnian paradigm shift away from a narrow focus on *p*-values as the criterion for whether findings merit publication, to be replaced by a more theory-driven approach, where tentative results from several studies (with preferably preregistered analysis plans) cumulatively lead to replicable, substantially tested claims.

combinations of words, how can they also "feel" and behave as if they are unitary lexical items? Their apparently dual, even paradoxical nature has led to a wide variety of analyses (for an overview, see Cappelle, 2023). Particle verbs also go to the heart of the falsifiability question raised by Hoffmann. In Cappelle (2006, 2009), I suggested that transitive particle verbs in English, used in *Did you turn off the TV?* or *Put the gun down!* fall under a general construction that does not specify anything about the order of the direct object NP relative to the particle (Prt). The "joined" verb-particle ordering (V Prt NP~Direct Object~) and the "split" ordering (V NP~Direct Object~ Prt) are then subsumed by this general construction as two more fully specified "allostructions." These allostructions are represented as being linked to each other, "horizontally" as we then say, to capture the incontestable fact there is a strong connection between them: speakers who hear a pseudo-combination in one ordering (e.g., *smurf off the TV*) can safely guess that this combination will also be possible in the other ordering (e.g., *smurf the TV off*). But, crucially, this relatedness is in fact already captured by representing each allostruction as a daughter of the same mother node (see Figure 3). And this also means that this node somehow resides in the minds of most if not all speakers of English – no minor presumption to make.

By contrast, for Audring (2019) and also for Hoffmann (2020) himself, no such general construction hovering over the two more specific ones seems to be needed as long as the two allostructions are linked to one another (see Figure 4). In this alternative constructional representation, co-indices in subscript are added to help us recover the corresponding elements across the two horizontally linked alternatives. This may seem a little unnecessary in this simple case, but co-indices become more obviously useful as representations are made more complex, including notably also semantic and prosodic information, as is done in the parallel architecture, a theoretical approach closely related to CxG (Jackendoff, 2010; Jackendoff & Audring, 2019). Information from other tiers than (morpho-)syntactic structure is left out here by Audring (2019), no doubt to allow easy comparison with Figure 3. The specification that the NP must be

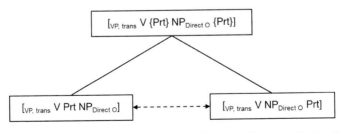

**Figure 3** Triangular constructional constellation with two allostructions and a mother node (based on Cappelle, 2006: 18).

**Figure 4** Purely horizontal constructional constellation with two allostructions and without a mother node (based on Audring, 2019: 281).

a direct object has also been intentionally omitted in her motherless representation, for reasons of readability.

Which, then, of the two constructional representations, Figure 3 or Figure 4, is most in line with the linguistic knowledge of competent speakers of English? According to Hoffmann (2020: 150), there doesn't seem to be any way to decide on this: "empirically, I would argue it is impossible to distinguish between the two analyses." Hoffmann does think that the mother node can be liquidated, as it doesn't uniquely sanction any specific "construct." That is, no transitive verb-particle combination found in usage can be licensed by the mother node without also being licensed by either of the two daughters. He therefore concludes: "as far as I can see, no data can ever be adduced to falsify its existence" (Hoffmann, 2020: 150).

Is it true that we can't rely on any observational facts by which we could either corroborate the independent existence of the mother node or argue against it? Let us consider three kinds of potential evidence, from psycholinguistics, computational modeling and introspective linguistic analysis.

## 4.1 Falsification by Psycholinguistic Evidence?

First, we could consider psycholinguistic evidence in the form of priming experiments, where we test how easily a string is recognized after a rapidly presented stimulus (e.g., Branigan et al., 1995). Unfortunately, we cannot expose test subjects to a syntactic schema. This isn't just because individuals who aren't linguists may not be familiar with grammatical category labels; even for linguists, a visual sequence of part-of-speech symbols is not at all the same thing as the putative mental schema such a string aims to represent. Therefore, a phrasal or clausal schema can only be tested via an instantiation in an actual phrase or clause.

As Ungerer (to appear: 12) observes, quite rightly to me, this makes it impossible to differentiate "vertical" priming from a schema to an instantiation and "horizontal" priming from one concrete string to another. Besides, the two horizontally linked instantiations in Figure 3 and Figure 4 are also of the schematic type, so these would have to be instantiated themselves by something lexically specific, too.

For the same reason, a sorting experiment of the kind used by Perek (2012) is incapable of distinguishing between the two (apparently) different constructional representations. I therefore concur with Ungerer, who writes: "As long as the psychological correlates of vertical and horizontal links can thus not be differentiated, the present account sides with Hoffmann's (2020: 150) view, cited above in the context of allostructions ... that vertical and horizontal models are empirically indistinguishable" (Ungerer, to appear: 12–13).

It is not that psycholinguistic experiments cannot arbitrate between *any* kind of vertical and horizontal relations. It would of course be possible, for instance, to test how well a word such as *apple* is primed by the word *fruit* (a more general word) and by the word *pear* (a word at the same level of specificity). The word *fruit* (/fruːt/) is a fully substantive item and can be presented visually or orally alongside other lexical items; it's just its meaning that is more "abstract" than that of *apple* or *pear*, and since it is not abstract in terms of its form, there is no obstacle to it being used as a stimulus. In the case of items with some formal abstraction, by contrast, there are as of yet no ways to circumvent their lack of full substance in an experiment.

In short, psycholinguistic testing does not seem to be an option to determine whether the mother schema in Figure 3 is needed over and above the two daughter schemas.

## 4.2 Falsification by Evidence from Computational Learning?

Second, if not to psycholinguistic experimentation, we could turn to statistical learning models, used in computational linguistics. Dunn (2017a, b) demonstrates how with the help of a complex algorithm, a multitude of potential construction grammars – note the plural – can be inductively learned from a large corpus (a couple of billion words from web-based sources). These grammars, Dunn (2017b) claims, can be falsified as well, if they then fail to predict which constructions are present in smaller subsets of that corpus. Falsifiability here is not a property of a single construction but of an entire set of constructions, a grammar. In fact, Dunn speaks of falsifiability as a property of CxG reformulated as a kind of automatic detection-and-sorting procedure (rather than as a theoretical framework for introspection), a mechanism Dunn (2017b) calls a "discovery device grammar," after an idea already exposed by Chomsky (1957). Chomsky's early conception of grammar along such lines was nicely (and intelligibly) summarized by Halliday (2003[1964]):

> According to [Chomsky's] well-known formulation, the grammar should provide a complete specification of an infinite set of grammatical sentences of the language, enumerating all sentences and no non-sentences, and

automatically assign to them structural descriptions. The theory should include a function for the evaluation of grammars, so that a choice can be made among different grammars all of which fulfill these requirements. The grammar can then be validated for compatibility with the given data and evaluated for relative simplicity . . . . (Halliday, 2003[1964]: 37)

There are clear echoes to Chomsky's hope for such a "lean mean grammar machine" when Dunn indicates that his work "develops a learning algorithm for selecting the optimum grammar out of the very large hypothesis space of potential grammars using a metric that balances both model coverage and model complexity." There are some notable differences, though. For Chomsky (1957), this discovery device got stuck in the conceptual phase and presumably wasn't meant to be actually built, but carrying out his proposals has meanwhile become an achievable project. Until quite late in the twentieth century, there was no way of determining which were the possible, well-formed sentences of a language and which ones were ill-formed, other than by using human judgment. The possible sentences were rightly seen as innumerable, and so putting the evaluation procedure for grammars to practice was beyond reach. The best one could do was try to find out whether some of the very partial proposals for grammar rules didn't allow any kinds of sentences that were clearly unacceptable, and, if they did, go back to the drawing board for better structural descriptions. With the event of large corpora, Chomsky's thought experiment (that we should conceive of grammar as a procedure for formulating multiple competing grammars that can be evaluated for maximum coverage and minimum clutter) can now be implemented. The infinity of possible sentences can be operationalized as "all the sentences that occur in a massive corpus": the size of a multi-billion-word corpus vastly exceeds the number of words an average person, by most estimates, will ever hear in their lifetime.[7]

Another important difference between Chomsky's early proposal and Dunn's work is that for Chomsky, structural descriptions of language consisted of syntactic symbols only, while in Dunn's approach, these can range from syntactic to lexical and they can be infused with meaning. Each potential construction grammar that Dunn's algorithm produces consists of a set of sequential patterns,

---

[7] Technical details are not important for our discussion here, but for completeness' sake, it should be pointed out that Dunn's algorithm doesn't use the entire 2-billion-word corpus all at once. For inductively learning and evaluating the potential grammars, the algorithm uses several smaller subsets. These subsets "represent multiple learners with the same Grammar learning the language from different inputs" (Dunn, 2017a: 258). From a theoretical point of view, it is interesting that a grammar that remains stable across subsets can spontaneously emerge in an inductive (data-driven), unsupervised fashion. It proves that "the [Chomskyan] hypothesis of innate structure is not required to explain relatively consistent grammars from different language learners" (Dunn, 2017a: 286).

also known as "n-grams" (that is, strings of *n* adjacent words, with n a natural number from two to five). Any given string of actual usage – take, for instance, *in the meantime* – can be represented in a variety of ways by means of n-grams. One kind of n-gram wholly consists of the lexical items used in it, in this case simply [*in the meantime*], which happens to be a familiar collocation. Another type of n-gram to describe the same string exclusively consists of part-of-speech categories, similar to the ones that Cappelle & Grabar (2016) extracted from COCA (Davies 2008–2019), in this case [Prep(osition) Det(erminer) N(oun)]. But there are also various hybrid representations, with lexical and syntactic items appearing next to each other (cf. Wible & Tsao, 2010; Lyngfelt et al., 2012; Forsberg et al., 2014), for instance [Prep *the meantime*], [*in* Det *meantime*], [*in the* N], or [*in* Det N], and so on. These learned n-grams can thus be of various degrees of specificity or generality, in line with the CxG idea that constructions can be maximally abstract schemas or fully item-specific sequences and that language users stock both types, and everything in-between, in one big storage space. Moreover, the algorithm can propose n-grams with one or more labels for phrasal constituents ([*in* NP] and [Prep NP]) and can even incorporate semantic information, whereby *meantime* might be marked as belonging to a particular conceptual domain of words. In a first version of the algorithm (Dunn, 2017a), the semantic labels were taken from an existing set of meaning tags, but in a later version (Dunn, 2017b), the meanings of lexical items were also inductively learned on the basis of their distribution in the corpus. (All words referring to time, for instance, will appear in much the same contexts, which is how we – or in this case, an automatic learner – can perceive them as being close in meaning to one another.) So, what makes Dunn's algorithm a truly CxG-inspired learning device is the wide range of possible n-grams: shorter or longer; purely lexical, purely syntactic or mixed; with or without constituents as slots; and with or without semantic information.

Some of these potential n-grams suggested by the machine are less interesting or meaningful than others, in the sense that they may represent the actual sequence itself but not any or many other sequences. Thus, including [Prep *the meantime*] or [*in* Det *meantime*] into the grammar might turn out quite pointless, as the preposition *in* and the determiner *the* are the only likely items to fill the variable slots in these sequences. The challenge of the learning algorithm is therefore to find patterns of the right grain size. The algorithm meets this challenge by "seek[ing] to maximize the coverage of the grammar while minimizing its size" (Dunn, 2017b: 5).

Now, as for our question about the existence of a mother node schematizing over the two variant structures in Figure 3, Dunn's discovery-device CxG unfortunately cannot provide an answer. One reason is that this mother node, as part of its *raison d'être*, does not specify the ordering of the particle relative to the direct object NP and as such doesn't have the form of any of the n-grams that could possibly be outputted by the algorithm. Another reason is that even if the algorithm were to be modified so as to include sequences underspecified for word order into its grammars, any grammar that contained such a structure in addition to its daughters would probably be weeded out – falsified, in other words – as it would not meet the requirement of being maximally parsimonious. When simplicity is built into the grammar selection procedure, a mother node that isn't any more productive (describing more utterances) than its two daughter nodes combined stands little chance of being part of any "optimal" grammar. The question, of course, is whether the human mind also works according to the demands of maximal simplicity. More generally, one may wonder whether computational learning is at all representative of how a human gets to arrive at a mental grammar, which, by the way, keeps evolving over the course of a person's life (Petré & Van de Velde, 2018; Anthonissen & Petré, 2019).

On the one hand, findings from inductive grammar learning algorithms such as Dunn's give us important insights into the learning of a grammar by humans, arbitrating between opposing theoretical views (innateness vs. emergentism). It also incorporates cognitive notions that have been central in CxG. For instance, the degree of entrenchment of a construction is operationalized as something computationally tractable, by means of various measures of association strength among the elements of a sequence. These measures seem perfectly valid proxies for what binds elements together into "chunks," "routines," "nodes in the network," or whichever other metaphor we want to use here.

On the other hand, a computer program operates in ways that would be hard to construe as mimicking the workings of a human brain or mind. For instance, when Dunn (2017b, 2) states that his computational method generates a "large number of potential grammars," he is referring to a great many alternatives indeed: "the algorithm produces a total hypothesis space of 1.5 million potential grammars" (Dunn, 2017b: 5). Needless to say, it is exceedingly unlikely that actual learners of a language hold so many different possible constructi-cons in their heads and then whittle down this "hypothesis space" to just one optimal constructi-con, or even just a few plausible, overlapping ones. Dunn fully recognizes that his computational learning algorithm is not a direct tool for psychological validation. Reflecting on the "actual" rather than "potential" constructions in the computationally learned optimum construction grammar, he writes:

> A final question here is whether these are posited to be psycholinguistically valid constructions. In other words, are the elements of this grammar supposed to be those present in the mind of a speaker of this language? The goal

here is somewhat more indirect: to automatically produce the inventory of constructions necessary to describe the corpus. The question is whether the algorithm can learn adequate grammatical representations from the corpus, not [whether] it necessarily learns exactly the same set as a human in exactly the same manner. (Dunn, 2017a: 279)

## 4.3 Falsification by "Evidence" from Introspective Linguistic Analysis?

We are thus faced with what looks like a deadlock: no psycholinguistic or computational modeling evidence seems to be available to distinguish between a layered and a flat representation for our particular case of structural variation (Figure 3 vs. Figure 4). The situation is not completely hopeless, though. I would argue that we can still use insights from a more introspective sort of linguistic analysis to try to see pros and cons of each option. This will not count as strong empirical evidence – and therefore maybe not as evidence at all – as no experiment or simulation is carried out. Various kinds of observational data, though, may (and should) play a role here, too, but these serve to *strengthen* the case for one position over another, rather than to settle the matter more or less definitively, and they combine with various kinds of argumentative considerations. I will here briefly show how such linguistic reasoning can be brought to bear on the issue at hand.

The representation in Figure 3 looks more complex than that in Figure 4, and Audring (2019) rightly argues that what is encoded in the mother node is also encoded by the lower-level sisters and the relation of connectedness they entertain. We might on that basis choose for the representation in Figure 4. But before committing "matricide" of the superordinate node, let us pause to think why such a single, general node might nonetheless have its purpose.

To me, a superordinate, underspecified schema seems like a valid candidate for a construction – a unit, remember, that is stored in the mind – in that it might be just that, and nothing more, that a speaker may access when in need of a particular lexical item that expresses an activity that can be performed on a patient argument. For instance, thinking of a laptop, a speaker might look for a word or expression that means something like "do something with it, with as a result that it is no longer off." A lexical item that might naturally present itself to this speaker would then be *turn on*, among a few alternatives (e.g., *flick on*, *flip on*, *open*, *switch on*).

If we take seriously the CxG idea that meaning and form are jointly present in linguistic units, we would then have to state what the morphosyntactic form is of this lexical item. Here, I think we can really make the case for a schema of a lexical item whose form is rather underspecified as to its integration in morphosyntax.

All that may have to be present at this general level are the elements *turn on* and the semantic information that there should be a patient of a certain kind. This lexical construction could be represented more or less as in (1):

(1)      [turn$_V$ on$_{Prt}$]
         Sem ACTIVATE < activator  something electric$_{e.g., \text{ computer, lights, TV}}$ >

From a great many other transitive particle verbs – and English does abound with them – a schema can emerge that is similarly morphosyntactically impre-cise, perhaps as in (2):

(2)      [V Prt]
         Sem ACT-UPON < agent    patient >

In other words, the suggestion here is that speakers are likely to have a mental representation of transitive particle verbs at a level that is syntactically rather impoverished, not telling them that the particle is either positioned right next to the verb or appears more distant from it, and not even saying anything about whether this unit is a verb or a verb phrase. Of course, we could quibble about the notational representation of this schema. Note that it has less information in it than the mother node in Figure 3. That is, the mother node for a transitive particle verb may not even need to have any specification of the two alternative word orders (indicated by a double appearance of the particle put in braces). There are several arguments for this.

### 4.3.1 Arguments for Underspecification
#### Too Much Information

Language users may access other kinds of lexical items, not just particle verbs, without having simultaneously a perfect idea of the syntactic ways of using them. Take the word *cat*. This by itself evokes a lot of meaning. If this is the case, there must be a mental representation for this word that houses this meaning. The form part, apart from the phonology (as well as the orthographical word image) of this lexical item, doesn't have to specify much beyond the fact that *cat* is a noun. There is no need to go into any rich detail about this noun, for example that it can be preceded by a determiner and form an NP, that there can be pre- and postmodification within that NP (*that scruffy cat of yours*), that an NP with *cat* can serve as Subject NP (*The cat is on the mat*) or as direct object (*So don't just blame the cat*), as Object of a Preposition (*Were you talking to the cat?*), and so on. All that is, no doubt, too much information when we just mentally behold the item *cat*.

By analogy, we can assume that a phrasal verb like *turn on* also exists at a level that isn't rich in syntactic detail. To be sure, the semantics of a verb is by its very nature more elaborate than that of a noun, in that it evokes participant roles, as is shown in (1). The point is, though, that this is information that can be represented in semantic, notional terms. No need for a speaker to see these participant roles already realized in all their (morpho-)syntactic detail.

## Demanding Daughters

Underspecification is all the more plausible because there are intricate structural differences between the two placement options, differences that are not represented in Figure 3 and Figure 4. In the joined ordering, the verb and the particle form a sort of complex verb, while when separated, the particle can head a full syntactic phrase. This is clear from the following pair of contrastive examples:

(3)      a.  *When I came home last night, I turned right on my laptop to check my email.
         b.  When I came home last night, I turned my laptop right on to check my email.

One might disagree with the strength of this judgment, but there is little doubt that (3b) is much more acceptable than (3a). In (3a), *turned right on* is problematic because one cannot disrupt the morphological unity of a word by inserting another lexical item.[8] In (3b), the particle is realized as a syntactic complement of the verb *turn*, just like the NP is one. As the head of a syntactic phrase, the particle can be modified by an adverb like *right*. In other words, the representations of the daughter nodes in Figure 3, and the two sisters in Figure 4, are a little too crude, in that they don't take into account the compound status of V-Prt in the adjacent structure and the status of the particle as head of a "particle phrase" (PrtP) in the discontinuous structure. Finer representations of each pattern could have been those in (4). I am using Audring's flat representation, using co-indices as in Figure 4:[9]

---

[8]  The appearance of an inflectional affix *-ed* on the verbal element shouldn't be taken as evidence that particle verbs like *turn on* cannot be compounds. Elsewhere in the constructi-con of English, compounds can, exceptionally, be left-headed, as shown by *brother(s)-in-law*, and receive an inflectional suffix on the head rather than at the end of the word. Only in a strict assembly-line conception of morphological derivation/compounding and inflection, where first the lexical item is formed and any inflectional suffix is then added on the outside of that finished item, would inflection in the middle of a word be problematic. In CxG, there can be a schema such as $[_V \text{V-Stem(-aff}_{infl}) \text{ Prt}]$.

[9]  The discontinuous structure specifies that the particle can in principle also be *followed* by material that belongs to the phrase it heads. For a particle verb such as *turn on*, one may be hard-pressed to find examples; in *turn the radio on to full volume*, for instance, the prepositional phrase *to full volume* is probably a separate constituent, an analysis supported by the fact that we can also say *turn on the radio to full volume*. However, for particle verbs with a "literal," directional meaning,

(4)     $[_{VP, \text{ trans}} [_V V_a \text{ Prt}_b] \text{ NP}_c]$ ——— $[_{VP, \text{ trans}} V_a \text{ NP}_c [_{\text{PrtP}} (\ldots) \text{ Prt}_b (\ldots)]]$

The daughters, in other words, are quite "demanding," stipulating that the particle has to be part of a compound or has to be a syntactic head. These are rather detailed morphosyntactic facts and one could imagine (without being able to prove) that the speaker doesn't need to have to care about them when simply looking for a lexical item to use with *my laptop*. A closer analysis of the two placement options thus reinforces the previous argument for the need of a more schematic, less worked-out node in the network.

This is not to say that speakers cannot store a lexical item like *turn on* as realized in one of the two orderings. Having heard the song *Fire* many times over, whose first line is *I'm ridin' in your car, you turn on the radio*, lots of language users will surely have built up a mental representation of *turn on* used in the joined structure. They may also have a stored representation of the discontinuous order (*turn . . . on*). If this is so, we might wonder again whether these two specific manifestation do not suffice by themselves after all for speakers to know how to use *turn on*. This brings us to a third consideration.

## More Specific Structures than Just Two

The two placement options shown in Figure 3 and Figure 4 do not exhaust the possibilities of how a transitive particle verb can be used. Consider the following authentic examples:

(5)     a.  The following scripts can be used to count the number of times a computer *has been turned on*.[10]
        b.  He told me to *turn on the radio loud* and jump all over the place. He said this would disrupt the bugging.[11]
        c.  McKenzie just *turned us some lights on*. That's probably better.[12]
        d.  . . . so went to move my car and it made a craaaazy noise (it started and it moved but it sounded a little bit like putting my mobile phone in the blender). So *off I turned it* and left it there.[13]

---

a post-particle PP can often more convincingly be treated as forming a single phrase with the particle (e.g., [*up to the sky*], [*right back down to earth*]). There are also many examples in which the particle can optionally be followed by an NP as complement (e.g., *put your hat on (your head)*), but if it is, we would normally call the particle a preposition, for right or for wrong. See Cappelle (2008) for details and relevant references.

[10] www.itsupportguides.com/knowledge-base/vbs-scripts/vbs-script-count-number-of-times-computer-has-turned-on/

[11] www.pressreader.com/south-africa/the-mercury-south-africa/20160608/281702613981727

[12] ne-np.facebook.com/guidedbygraceboutique/videos/heyyyy-yall-join-us-for-a-fun-thursday-live-/445647074126771/

[13] forums.moneysavingexpert.com/discussion/3099580/cam-belt-has-gone-on-my-car-not-sure-what-to-do

Sentence (5a) uses the lexical item *turn on* in the passive; (5b) uses it with an adjectival predicative complement following the direct object NP; in (5c), we have an extra benefactive NP (i.e., this sentence uses a kind of ditransitive construction); in (5d), the particle is preposed, a placement that is possible because the particle has sufficient semantic content independently of the verb (Cappelle, 2002), as is evident from the concept of an *on/off button*. Such sentences show that the two daughters (or motherless sisters) represented in Figure 3 and Figure 4 are only two syntactic realizations of the transitive verb-particle construction. Note that, while the addition of a predicative or benefactive constituent is rare, as is preposing, the passive isn't at all uncommon. Audring (2019: 283) herself argues that with an increasing number of types, the likelihood of there being a mother schema generalizing over them also increases. Evidence of a larger number of structural types than initially thought, given by the examples in (5a–d), would thus speak in favor of a mother construction holding the family together.

Alternatively, it may be the case that the two allostructional daughters have themselves several daughters, which pushes the problem a level further down: Is there even a schematic "joined" verb-particle construction, or should we consider the different structural possibilities of the joined alternative (used in the passive, used with a predicative complement, etc.) as ever so many sisters that miss a mother node above them? And, similarly, is there even a schematic "split" verb-particle construction, or are there only several split verb-particle sisters? But if that were the case, the existence of an overarching mother node to cover all joined and all split uses would only become more likely. Without any lower-level generalizations, the number of types that all have something in common (namely, the presence of a particle, a verb, and a patient argument) would then seem sufficiently large for a schema to emerge that represents this commonality.

### 4.3.2 A Schema and a Horizontal Link Are Notational Variants

To be sure, one could *still* argue that there is nothing that prevents the view that the examples in (5a–d) merely show that there are just more sisters around and that these could all be motherless. But let us think this possibility through. If they don't have a shared mother, how exactly are they connected among themselves? That is, would recognizing more sisters necessarily mean that each of these extra nodes in the network is (horizontally) linked to each of the other nodes?

We could assume the verb phrase in (5b) to have been sanctioned by the template [[V Prt] NP AdjP]. This template is more similar to the canonical joined allostruction than to the canonical split allostruction. (The "canonical" verb-particle patterns are the two allostructions shown in Figure 3 and Figure 4:

they are default options, without any embellishments, so to speak.) By contrast, a template like [V NP$_{Benef}$ NP Prt], responsible for (5c), is closely linked to the canonical split ordering, not to the canonical joined ordering. Observe that there is also a pattern with an extra predicative complement displaying the split ordering (e.g., *turn the radio on loud*) and that the joined and split particle verb schemas with a predicative complement would be naturally linked to each other (both having such a predicative phrase) but not to the pattern with a benefactive NP (both lacking such a phrase). Likewise, the pattern with an extra benefactive NP also appears in the "joined" ordering. (Note, though, that as the benefactive element can only really be realized as a pronoun, this pronoun will appear as a clitic to the verb, separating it from the particle, but the direct object NP does follow the particle, as in *Hey boy, run over there and turn me on that TV.*)[14] Again, the two word orders with a benefactive would be linked to each other, but not to the two mutually linked patterns with the predicative phrase. As for the passive, we could assume that there is both a version that is linked to the joined ordering, where the verb and the particle are felt to be a compound (something like [NP BE [V-*en* Prt]]), and a version linked to the split ordering, where the particle is syntactically more independent of the verb (something like [NP BE V-en PrtP]). (There would then be structural ambiguity in (5a), but not in, for instance, *The LEDs were turned right off again*, where the particle clearly appears as the head of a phrase.) The preposing pattern in (5d), finally, can only be seen as linked with the discontinuous ordering, as only syntactic phrases can be preposed, not parts of compounds.

If we were to plot these correspondences on a single taxonomical plane, we would naturally see a family resemblance network with some clusters emerging (see Figure 5). The figure looks at a network "from above," so a node in a higher position in this figure is not to be interpreted as a more general schema than a lower node.

How, now, are these clusters different from local generalizations? Observe that such a network allows us to answer questions such as: Is a joined particle verb with a benefactive NP more similar to a split particle verb with a benefactive NP than to a split particle verb with a predicative complement?

---

[14] The example used here is an authentic one found on tigerdroppings.com/rant/o-t-lounge/hulk-hogans-admits-his-kids-turn-him-on/97652812/page-5/, where it was apparently used as part of an elaborate linguistic pun (but there is nothing to doubt that its acceptability is questionable for that reason). Though the pattern is rare, further examples can be found (e.g., *gonna turn me on some music and relax*). Authentic examples in which the benefactive is a full NP are hard to come by, but such an NP would also separate the verb and the particle, regardless of the position of the particle relative to the direct object (e.g., *This event will give [these people] back some dignity / This event will give [these people] some dignity back*).

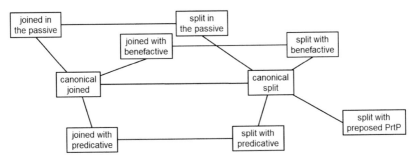

**Figure 5** "Top view" of a simple network in which various constructional schemas involving transitive particle verbs are nodes positioned on the same taxonomical plane.

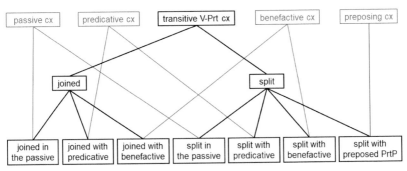

**Figure 6** Taxonomically organized representation of a simple network of various constructional schemas involving transitive particle verbs (in black and with thick outlines and connections). Also shown are independently existing constructions which specific (pairs of) constructions also inherit from (in gray and with thinner outlines and connections; greyscale and thickness are not meant to reflect strength of entrenchment and strength of connection).

If the network represents similarities perceived by actual language users – still an empirical issue, though – the answer can be read off it: yes. Such graded similarities can also be represented efficiently and conventionally in a taxonomical network with multiple inheritance (see Figure 6).

In a sense, Figure 6 can be seen as the "front view" of the network shown in Figure 5. The only nodes not shown here are the canonical joined and split verb-particle constructions, essentially for lack of space. Rather than having only horizontal links between (some of) the lower nodes, the clusters are represented by means of mid-level schemas that are "relational hubs" (cf. Audring, 2019: 283). Each of the low-level schemas is thus bound to a single more general node rather than to each of its sisters (or rather than to a single "most normal" sister within its cluster). The two mid-level schemas in Figure 5, "joined" and "split," aren't as specific as the two allostructional nodes in Figure 3 and Figure 4: they are instantiated by the passive, for instance, which is not a VP but a clause-level construction.

I recently voiced my strong suspicion that the representations in Figure 3 and Figure 4 are just notational variants of each other: "as far as I can see, Audring's 'flat' representation and my 'triangular' one aren't different in any cognitively crucial way" (Cappelle et al., 2021: 282). Endorsement for this view can be found in Ungerer's (to appear) paper on the topic, which in a nutshell states this:

> The present proposal is thus *that vertical and horizontal links do not encode distinct cognitive mechanisms, but that they constitute notational variants for representing constructional similarities.* On this account, schemas contain the shared features of the subtypes over which they generalise; these shared features can alternatively be represented by horizontal similarity links. ... [A] horizontal link between two constructions is equivalent to a constellation of a schema node plus the two vertical links that relate the schema to its subtypes. (Ungerer, to appear: 14)

Not every CxGian may agree with this position. Saying that every horizontal relation also implies a vertical one would mean that one is prepared to accept that for paired sister words like *ambition* and *ambitious*, there is also a mother, even though the base they share does not occur as a free morpheme. This might not seem very attractive. In any case, Jackendoff & Audring (2020, 6) dispel for these words the possibility of an abstract construction (which would let the non-lexical base and the meaning of "desire" to be inherited but which would have an open affix position), adding that it is "not an optimal solution." However, nothing needs to be *inherited* from this node: it could simply exist as an emergent entity, derived from the sister items. Furthermore, in terms of representational efficiency, a mother node could assist the linguist in discerning the shared characteristics between two sister nodes by displaying only those shared aspects, without any extraneous information.

### 4.3.3 An Analogy to Argue against Pure Analogy

*If* my mother-plus-daughters representation and Audring's horizontal-link-only representation are, ultimately, not cognitively different, one might wonder: So, what's all the fuss about? I think the correct question to ask is not whether the mother node in Figure 3 is justified but whether it represents a stable node in the speaker's network of constructions. With respect to Audring's representation, that question would translate as to whether the horizontal line represents a connection which has some permanence or whether it arises only on an ad hoc, as-needed basis. In other words, the question is *not* whether we can falsify the mother node and only keep the horizontally linked schemas – as this is a false choice – but whether, regardless of the representation, the similarity between the two allostructions is perceived only temporarily or whether the two allostructions are firmly joined in cognition (and thus together form a complex cluster in the contructi-con, however we want to represent it diagrammatically).

To answer this question, we might want to draw an analogy with a nonlinguistic situation. Imagine a car mechanic who has intimate familiarity with front-wheel drive cars, such as a Toyota Corolla, a Honda Accord, a Chevrolet Malibu, a Volvo S60 and many others. The car mechanic probably has a mental image of what a front-wheel-drive car is like, including the knowledge that the engine is under the hood in the front of the car. Suppose furthermore that our car mechanic is also often asked by owners of rear-wheel-drive cars to do some repairing or tuning job to their Porsche 911, Jaguar X11, BMW 3, original Volkswagen Beetle, and others. Again, it is highly likely that the mechanic has a cognitive representation of such kind of cars. Curiously, though, what is lacking in the mechanic's cognition is the concept of a car in general.

Sounds absurd? It should. By analogy, it should also strike us as highly implausible that speakers do not have a schema for the (transitive) verb-particle construction even if they have schemas for the joined and for the split subconstructions. The absurdity of this is heightened by the observation that there are several constructions – the passive, the predicative construction, the benefactive construction – that apply to both alternatives. This shows that the two alternatives, even if they have their own specificities (not mentioned here, but relating for instance to information packaging), show many similarities, just like both front-wheel-drive and back-wheel-drive cars may be convertibles, may be fitted with an extra spoiler, and so on. Thus, these other constructions make us realize that we are dealing with a single closely-knit category, not two hardly linked schemas. The unrelatedness of the two alternatives is falsified by those several schematic constructions that can interact with both of them. In addition, there are of course several hundreds of common particle verbs that language users have seen or heard in both patterns.

For an *individual* transitive verb-particle combination, it is imaginable that a mother node can be constructed without staying in the grammar. For instance, on hearing *clap on the lights* ("turn on the lights by means of wireless clap activation"), a language user could "provisionally" form a syntactically under-specified [*clap*$_V$ *on*$_{Prt}$] schema, which, when perceived as an instance of the [V Prt] schema in (2), would then sanction the alternative ordering *clap the lights on* (because the general [V Prt] schema is linked to both ordererings). If such a lexical mother node is formed at all, it would not reach any significant level of entrenchment. The formation of an ad hoc mother node is not easily distinguishable from analogization, a process that completely bypasses such a mother node:

(6)      [*turn on* NP] : [*turn* NP *on*] : : [*clap on* NP] : _____

(The single colon in (6) stands for "is to" and the double colon for "just as.") Thus, language users can probably rely on the known alternation between the joined and split version of the combination *turn on* to "compute" or "coin" the split version of *clap on* when that version is called for, for instance when the NP is the pronoun *them*.

While it is admittedly not clear whether a higher-order node needs to be created for one-off uses like this, a motherless scenario has been argued above to be wildly unrealistic when it comes to the maximally general joined and split V-Prt alternatives. These alternatives exhibit too many similarities for them not to be linked via a single schema. Besides, when a form is created by analogy only, the horizontal link may not be "entrenched" either, so not building a mother node is equivalent here again to not having a durable horizontal connection.

## 4.4 Interim Summary

We have seen that psycholinguistic testing via priming experiments and computational modeling cannot argue for or against a mother node that has two daughters that jointly cover an area of language use. However, we can adduce linguistic arguments to demonstrate that *not* having an underspecified schema would fly in the face of plausibility:

- speakers may want to think about a lexical item *in abstracto*, without having to worry (yet) about any instructions of how to use it (much like the lexical entry for a word like *cat* has little syntax about it);
- in addition, the subschemas regulating the morphosyntactic realization of that lexical item could impose constraints that are just too specific to be relevant;
- closer linguistic analysis can reveal that there are more ways of using lexical items of a particular class than just two, and the more ways there are (especially if these don't differ that much one from the other), the more likely the existence of a schema.

Moreover, linking patterns horizontally in a visual representation is a notational variant of creating a mother node above them: these visualizations do not stand for cognitively different mechanisms. When there is a broad range of independently existing constructions that can combine with instances of one subschema just as well as with instances of the other, these additional constructions effectively highlight the absurdity of the two subschemas not being linked.

In short, with the help of careful linguistic observation and analysis, we have been able to test and refute the view that two alternating constructional schemas are *not* subsumed under a more general mother node – or *not* joined by a permanent horizontal link, which comes down to the same thing.

We may be relieved that a contentious proposal made within CxG turns out "testable," mostly by consideration of relevant linguistic facts and the force of reasoning. The seemingly rival proposal isn't much different after all, and the *real* alternative – which is that the constructions concerned are not linked in cognition in any stable way – can be refuted as absurd.

So far, so falsifiable. But what about the theory itself?

## 5 How Construction Grammar Could Play the Science Game Fairly

> [T]he worst that Construction Grammarians could do would be to look the other way, towards nice meaningful patterns such as THE X-ER THE Y-ER or the WAY construction, and pretend that the problem of meaningless constructions does not exist.
>
> (Hilpert, 2019: 68)

A watertight theory that can withstand any possible counterargument might look attractive to its adherents. However, when it is in effect unfalsifiable, because no empirical data can be adduced against it, its value as a scientific theory is diminished. Detractors of the theory will feel justifiably frustrated by the impossibility to have a genuine, constructive discussion when no single observable fact at all seems to have the effect of invalidating the theory in the eyes of those who believe in it.

Figure 7 represents this failing dialectic in cartoon form. The target of the scorn here is not CxG but generative linguistics, which believes in the existence of UG as a common blueprint for all languages. The short dialogues summarize some of the usual usage-based counterarguments to UG reviewed here and how these are brushed off as irrelevant. The use of this comic strip format instead of a more conventional diagrammatic figure will be felt, I hope, to suitably reproduce the truly often cartoonish nature of cross-theoretical discourse, which is rife with accusations, from each side in fact, that one's positions have been grossly, even grotesquely, misconstrued by the other side.

The setting of the conversations in Figure 7 is an "unlikely" conference, in that research communities as widely different as usage-based linguistics and the UG-oriented approach rarely interact (cf. also Section 2.2). Newmeyer (1998: 1–5) provides a similar but more extensive "(not totally) imaginary dialogue" between Sandy Forman and Chris Funk – made-up names that should give

**Figure 7** An xkcd-style cartoon representation of some major usage-based counterarguments to the UG approach and how these are, in turn, countered. Dismissing any piece of counterevidence as irrelevant does not prove the superiority of one's theory when it thereby becomes clear that this theory is, effectively, unfalsifiable. (Created with Comix I/O)

a clue as to their theoretical allegiance.[15] After their debate, spanning four and a half pages, Newmeyer (1998: 5–6) comments: "If there is anything unrealistic about their exchange, it is the fact that it could have taken place at all! Few functionalists and fewer still formalists are aware enough of the positions taken by the other side (caricatures of those positions aside) to make possible the back-and-forth to which we have just been exposed." This said, commenting on my cartoon in Figure 7, Ben Ambridge (p.c.) let me know: "I've actually had the third exchange almost word-for-word at a conference!" This assures me that despite their exaggerated representation, these exchanges are at least somewhat realistic and relatable.

There is a rich – but, as we pointed out in Section 2.1, somewhat dwindling – tradition in CxG publications to contrast one's own theory with research in the Chomskyan camp, which was dominant for many decades. For just one example of this CxG-vs-generative-linguistics trope, see Sag, Boas, and Kay (2012: 1). It is not my intention to encourage a revival of this practice. Of course, my insinuation that Chomskyan UG-oriented linguistics has become unfalsifiable can be interpreted as implying that CxG is the scientifically better alternative. Proving one theory wrong or unfalsifiable, however, is not tantamount to proving the other one right or falsifiable. Things are not *that* easy, as it is not the case that the two theories take exactly opposite positions. They also have different objectives, which makes it hard and even impossible to say that if one theoretical option is valid, then by that very fact, the other is not. Chomskyan linguistics and cognitive linguistics could be considered incommensurable, in the sense of Kuhn (2012[1962]), because they represent fundamentally different approaches to studying language. Their underlying assumptions, research methodologies, and concepts are so distinct that meaningful dialogue between the two paradigms becomes challenging. This is what the cartoon tries to capture.

Rather than viewing the cartoon as a way of triumphing over generative linguistics, it should be read as a cautionary tale for CxG. For a theory to be respectable, there should be sufficient clarity as to what it is about, its undergirding premises should be valid or at least somewhat commonsensical, and its proponents should demonstrate a preparedness to abandon or modify the theory in the face of sufficiently serious counterexamples to its basic claim. Modification is only a suitable option if it doesn't change the theory beyond all recognition and if it doesn't just serve to protect the hard core of the theory without leading to any new insights. In that case, it would have become a pseudoscientific, "degenerating" research program (Lakatos, 1978: 5).

---

[15] Hollmann (2022), too, provides an imaginary conversation about usage-based and generative grammar. His is more probable and less vexing, as it is between a student of linguistics and a professional linguist.

When the central claim of the theory starts becoming explanatorily vacuous and no longer has any obvious relation to what the discipline is meant to be concerned with – the study of spoken or signed languages – one should be ready to leave the "theory" behind. These are intended to be more than thinly veiled criticisms of the UG approach. The question is, though: Can CxG do better?

If CxG is to play the science game fairly – more fairly than its former main rival – it should follow the following three rules:

1. Be very clear on what the scope of the theory is, what its goals are, and avoid any ambiguity or vagueness about what its major, strongest assumption is.
2. Be ready to revise some of its secondary, auxiliary assumptions, if these turn out not to be fully accurate.
3. Actively search not just for findings that confirm the central assumption but also, crucially, for the kind of research outcomes that would undermine it.

## 5.1 Clearly State the Object and the Objective

We saw in Section 1.3 that CxG can be captured in a number of tenets or basic ideas (Figure 1). Falsifying the theory – or attempting to do so – is hard if it is not clear what its most central and distinctive claim is. We must therefore make sure that to outsiders, and also to adherents, there is as little misunderstanding as possible regarding its essence. The following passage provides some answers as to the question what CxG really is a theory of:

> Construction Grammar is a theory of language that focuses on what constitutes linguistic knowledge. Knowing a language, it is argued, only (or mostly) consists in knowing the constructions in that language (hence the name of the theory). Like the Saussurean sign, constructions are defined as conventional units that combine a specific form with (one or more) semantic and discourse functional properties (Goldberg 1995, 2006). And one of the major claims of the theory has always been that not only morphemes, words or idioms have constructional status (i.e., conventionally associate a form with a meaning), but that the larger syntactic structures in which they occur are also constructions with their own semantic or discourse functions (Goldberg 2003:221). (Leclercq, 2019: 273–274)

This characterization of the theory is in line with what can be found in various up-to-date presentations (e.g., Hilpert, 2019; Hoffmann, 2022). It only states what CxG takes as its object of study, though, and not what the goal is of the theory, or set of theories. For this, we are informed by Goldberg (2013):

> Constructionist approaches aim to account for the full range of facts about language, without assuming that a particular subset of the data is part of a privileged "core." (Goldberg, 2013: 219).

In some respect, Goldberg's statement doesn't sound all that different from Chomsky's (1965: 27–28) formulation of the goal of linguistic theory (see also Langacker, 2005b: 158–160). Notice in Goldberg's formulation the use of *account for* (cf. Chomsky's *develop an account of*), which here, as I see it, is not used in the sense of "explain" but more in the sense of "provide an enumerative description or overview of."

At a very general level, CxG doesn't so much attempt to explain or predict phenomena as try to be descriptively adequate, using a coherent terminological and conceptual apparatus. Müller (2023: 316) formulates the goal of CxG as follows: "The aim of Construction Grammar is to both describe and theoretically explore language in its entirety." I agree that CxG is often more about exploration of uncharted territory than about explanation of previously observed data.

Importantly, though, constructionist approaches aim to record not just what is universal about languages, if anything, but also what is specific to individual languages. And in doing so, these approaches do not restrict their attention to what is regular in a language but also, or especially, focus on what is idiosyncratic and bizarre in it, something which has led to the reproach that CxGians are mainly interested in "collecting butterflies" (cf. Perek, 2021: s.p.).[16] Focusing on the irregular is a justified choice, however, the motivation being that if we can handle what's hard, then we should also be able to handle what's comparatively easy. (See Culicover & Jackendoff, 2005: 25–37; Müller, 2023: 541–543, for discussion of the problem of making a distinction between "core" and "periphery.")

This ambitious goal of CxG remains rather vague. For lack of a single clear general prediction, it is not clear yet, from its mission statement quoted above, what could be the sort of evidence that proves CxG wrong. In this respect, there is a laudably succinct statement of CxG's central claim in the blurb of Hilpert's (2019) textbook:

> The central and radical claim of Construction Grammar is that linguistic knowledge can be fully described as knowledge of constructions, which are defined as symbolic units that connect a linguistic form with meaning. (Hilpert, 2019, from the publisher's website)

This, at least, has the advantage that it not only makes reference to the domain of study (our knowledge of language) and that it includes a definition of

---

[16] Some CxGians even wallow in the activity of what Desagulier (2017: 7) refers to as "chasing butterflies," that is, the practice of deliberately running queries in a corpus (or a web browser) "in search of a savory example."

construction (as being a form-function pairing) but also that it is a maximally bold proposition: no aspect of our linguistic knowledge is *not* describable as knowledge of constructions.

## 5.2 Reconsider Some Auxiliary Assumptions

The premises we adopt shouldn't just serve to save the core idea of our theory. Unfortunately, this may be the case to some extent in CxG. If the most central, boldest claim of CxG is that all of our knowledge of language is made up of constructions, of whatever size and complexity (cf. also Goldberg's first and seventh tenets combined and Hilpert's basic idea #1 in Figure 1), then this claim is protected by some assumptions without whose acceptance it becomes less intuitively correct and thus more vulnerable.

### 5.2.1 Domain-Generality

An alternative definition of constructions is not so much as form-meaning units but as certain mental categories we form: "constructions are first and foremost something cognitive, that is, a piece of speakers' linguistic knowledge. More specifically, we can say that a construction is a generalisation that speakers make across a number of encounters with linguistic forms" (Hilpert, 2019: 26).[17] To the extent that a construction is understood as a mental category, it can be advantageous to the theory to argue that the way humans acquire these categories, how and where they store them and how they retrieve them for use is not essentially different from how they learn, remember and handle other bits of knowledge – bits that are not linguistic in nature. But is linguistic cognition that 'ordinary'?

It would not be entirely inaccurate to characterize the current theoretical landscape as being made up of two radically opposite views of language, advocated by two competing schools: cognitive linguistics (Evans & Green, 2002; Geeraarts & Cuyckens, 2007; Dąbrowska & Divjak, 2015; Ungerer & Schmid, 2006; Dancygier, 2021; Xu & Taylor, 2021) and biolinguistics (Hauser, Chomsky, & Fitch, 2002; Chomsky, 2007, 2017; Berwick & Chomsky, 2016; Crain, Koring, & Thornton, 2017). Both of these theoretical perspectives claim to present a cognitively plausible view of language, but these views are fundamentally different.

Cognitive linguistics is interested in various functional aspects of language. It places a strong emphasis on pragmatic competence, views our linguistic knowledge as intertwined with general cognition, and draws parallels between our acquisition of language and our emergent acquisition of nonlinguistic

---

[17] Page references here and elsewhere to Hilpert (2019) are to the electronic version. The page numbers may differ from those in the printed book.

categories. Construction Grammar was born from the womb of cognitive linguistics – Lakoff (1987) is a standard reference to both – and has inherited from it the assumption that linguistic cognition is not qualitatively different from extralinguistic cognition.

Biolinguistics, in its broadest possible sense, is concerned with understanding the biological foundations of human language, including its evolution, neurological and genetic basis, acquisition, and how language compares to communication systems in other species. In fact, though, Biolinguistics is also, as was briefly noted in Section 2.1, an outgrowth of Chomsky's minimalist program (Chomsky, 2000; 2015[1995]). It focuses on the formal side of language and assumes that all of our crucial language knowledge is available from birth – not just, as is sufficiently known about Chomsky's theory, the general syntactic rules but also, less well known, "a structured inventory of possible lexical items" (Chomsky, 2005: 4). That Chomsky lays claim to advancing a *bio*-linguistic perspective to language is due to his well-known view that the language faculty results from "a genetic endowment, apparently nearly uniform for the species" (Chomsky, 2005: 6). Chomsky has long put forward the existence of a "language-acquisition device" (Chomsky, 1965: 32, 47), which enables children to sift through all the possible grammars in the world until they settle on one that is most in accordance with the one they hear being used around them (see, e.g., Yang, 2002, for a specific proposal along those lines approved of by Chomsky).

The idea that there is an inborn and specialized system for language is anathema to cognitive linguistics. As Tomasello et al. (2005) observe, humans are very good at reading communicative intentions, both in speech and in other forms of interactions. Cognitive linguists believe that with our current understanding of how children construct grammar knowledge (e.g., Tomasello, 2006), we needn't assume that they bring to this task any elaborate a priori knowledge of structural constraints on the language to be learned. Sure, all members of our species share a capacity for language – what Haspelmath (2020) calls a human "linguisticality" (by analogy with *musicality*). When Tomasello (2009) nevertheless proclaimed that "Universal Grammar is dead," it is because commonalities across the world's languages, he argued, are derivable from prelinguistic, "universal aspects of human cognition, social interaction and information processing" (Tomasello, 2009: 471). Our genetically provided language endowment may simply involve the effortless – dare we say, instinctive – attention children pay to the noises made by their parents and other caregivers. A natural sensitivity to recursive properties of language – which for Chomsky is essential to language – may feature in this capacity. For cognitive linguists, though, it just isn't obvious why this ability should be specifically linguistic rather than domain-general.

Universal grammar, if we want to call it that, might be invoked merely to explain why children are so *good* at detecting the meaningful bits in spoken (or signed) signals. The position that many types of domain-general mechanisms come into play in linguistic cognition is not incompatible, cognitive linguists argue, with the possibility that our capacity for language is hardwired in our brains as part of our genetic constitution (Broccias, 2013: 192). Yet, "Cognitive Linguistics" (with or without capital letter) derives its name from stressing the generality of those cognitive processes, that is, their being language-independent. Statements like the following are typical of this view:

> Cognitive Linguistics does not adhere to the presumption (common in other linguistic frameworks) that there is a single "universal grammar" underlying all languages. . . . Cognitive Linguistics assumes only that linguistic cognition is part of overall cognition and behaves in the same way. (Janda, 2007: 54)

> Insofar as possible, linguistic structure is seen as drawing on other, more basic systems and abilities (e.g., perception, memory, categorization) from which it cannot be segregated (Langacker, 2008: 8).

Bybee (2010, 2012), notably, has argued for the relevance to language of "domain-general processes of [warning: long list coming up – B.C.] cross-modal association (which gives us form-meaning relations), categorization, chunking, neuro-motor automatization, rich memory, inference and analogy" (Torrent, 2012: 3). Similar views have also been made by Christiansen and Chater (2008).

The view that domain-general processes form the basis of grammar is a mantra in cognitive linguistics but is also an idea close to the heart of CxGians. Thus, Goldberg (2006), while again not denying that humans have a unique capacity for language, appears to doubt that there is anything cognitively specific about it:

> The question is not whether anything at all is specific to human beings and/or hard wired into the brain, but whether there exist rules that are specific to human language and not a result of our general conceptual/perceptual apparatus together with our experience of the world. (Goldberg, 2006: 188)

As Goldberg (1995: 5; 2006: 59) formulates it most succinctly: "knowledge of language is knowledge." It is this view that is discernible in the fourth, fifth, and sixth tenets (left) and basic idea #10 (right) in Figure 1. In Pulvermüller, Cappelle, and Shtyrov (2013), the view that language is co-extensive with general cognitive abilities was also defended:

> [W]e have mentioned neurobiological mechanisms for abstracting rulelike combinatorial mechanisms from linguistic utterances and, therefore, we submit that "syntactic" structures need not be pre-installed in the brain;

they can arise gradually on the basis of combinations of words that the
language user encounters. This supports the usage-based outlook on language
learning shared by cognitive-linguistic and constructionist approaches.
(Pulvermüller, Cappelle, & Shtyrov, 2013: 410)

Now, while we may not come onto this world with a set of syntax rules, let us still
keep it as an open, empirical question whether the regions in our brain that are
involved with language processing and production are the same regions that carry
out nonlinguistic tasks. Note the important "insofar as possible" hedge in
Langacker's quote above: a careful cognitive-linguistic and constructionist position is one which allows for the possibility that not everything about language is
a matter of how the mind or brain *generally* deals with complex phenomena.

Diachek and colleagues (2020) review thirty different brain imaging experiments, scrutinizing the results of 678 fMRI (functional Magnetic Resonance
Imaging) scanning sessions conducted with 481 unique participants. This review
study demonstrates that general-purpose cognitive resources housed in bilateral
fronto-parietal areas are only recruited when participants are asked to carry out
a true experimental task on top of the input stimuli, such as rating a sentence or
judging its plausibility (e.g., of *The cop arrested the criminal* vs. *The criminal
arrested the cop*; Ivanova et al. 2021). However, this domain-general network is
not active above a baseline in experiments in which participants had to engage
more passively in ordinary linguistic activities, such as simply reading or hearing
sentences. Even aspects of comprehension that could be thought – and had been
claimed – to involve a great deal of this domain-general processing apparently do
not require areas beyond the language-specific network. Such aspects include
inhibiting irrelevant parses of sentences, guessing upcoming words or structures,
and keeping words active until their meaning falls into place later in a sentence,
and so on. The authors' aggregated findings thus undermine the view that
domain-general executive brain resources (those involved generally in working
memory, setting and monitoring of goals, and other forms of cognitive control)
play a role when we engage in certain naturalistic sentence comprehension tasks,
cognitively demanding though these are.

This and related research (e.g., Fedorenko, Behr, & Kanwisher 2011; Blank
& Fedorenko, 2017; Campbell & Tyler, 2018) would suggest that there is
a language-related brain component after all – "all the core linguistic computa-
tions take place outside of MD [the 'multiple-demand,' domain-general net-
work] areas, presumably in the language-selective areas" (Diachek et al., 2020:
4546). Fedorenko and Thompson-Schill (2014) invite us to think of a language
network in the brain that has a core for lexical access and combinatorial
processing and a domain-general periphery that only sometimes interacts with
the language area. This, then, may possibly lend some support to the idea that

our capacity for language as a *sui generis* cognitive system does have some cognitive reality. It would seem that we are endowed with a faculty in the mind that is specialized for dealing with language-processing tasks. These recent findings can, tentatively, be taken to challenge the CxG assumption that language merely and exclusively draws on domain-general processes.

I add *tentatively* as we may not yet have reached the point where we fully understand the theoretical significance of these findings. Perhaps one should not confuse the existence of a language-dedicated faculty (or even just some language-specific areas) with the cognitive operations applied to language. Thus, one might potentially consider that language-related operations take place in the brain in areas that are specifically dedicated to language but that some of these processes (abstraction, categorization, attention, etc.) are ones that we also find in other areas.

We have to be careful, in any case, not to succumb to any all too slogan-like story about the relatedness (or worse, identity) of linguistic and nonlinguistic cognition. This shouldn't be an all-or-nothing matter. We don't have to make a forced choice between the view that *everything* about language is handled by the mind or brain in exactly the same way as nonlinguistic experiences, and the totally opposite view that *nothing* about how the mind or brain deals with language is similar to how it processes experiences in other domains. There are middle positions, for instance one whereby syntactic integration of linguistic entities is recognized as a language-specific cognitive skill that cannot easily be reduced to anything else, while the way we learn the meanings of words and acquire whole-sentence routines is not that different from how we categorize purely visual objects, or become good at playing a riff on a guitar through practice.

Construction grammarians, in fact, might not like such a middle view, as it would suggest a strong dissociation of syntactic assembly from lexical access and semantic processing. Perhaps the lesser of two "evils" is to give up the domain-generality of language, rather than a radical rift between syntax and semantics. It may be seen as comforting, therefore, that findings reported by Fedorenko and colleagues (2020) suggest that syntactic, combinatorial processing and lexico-semantic processing appear to be deeply interconnected in the brain, challenging the idea that they rely on distinct neural mechanisms, and highlighting a stronger emphasis on meaning rather than pure syntactic form in language processing. See also Pulvermüller, Cappelle, and Shtyrov (2013: 410–411) for the view that the interconnectedness of syntax and semantics, commonly found in cognitive-linguistic and constructionist grammar approaches, can be effectively represented within a neurobiological model in which cell assemblies representing (classes of) lexical items bind to higher-order neuronal circuits that regulate which kinds of items go together with which others.

We should also not cling to a simplistic "language is cognitively ordinary" or an equally simplistic "language is cognitively special" view without being clear on which domains within the study of language we're talking about. Importantly, are we discussing language structure (existing grammar regularities and constraints) or language processing (how we fit words and structures together in production and unpack them in comprehension)? Or is it acquisition we have in mind? Or language change? Structure and processing may involve different kinds of processes, even though these aspects are strongly related, notably by the universal impetus for languages to be efficient, that is, to make both speakers/signers and receivers save effort during communication (cf. Levshina & Moran, 2021). Acquisition and change will likely involve different sets of factors still, some of them more social and cultural.

The main point is this. As CxGians, we may be highly skeptical about much of Chomsky's "biolinguistic" program, and for good reasons. Especially its neglect of the functional, communicative aspect of language is suspect. Cognitive linguists have opposed with great zeal the generative-linguistic idea that there is an encapsulated language module and have emphasized instead that language is not at all detached from our general cognitive abilities. Domain-generality is a shibboleth by which we recognize cognitive linguists and CxGians, but we shouldn't be too fanatical about it. Let's not be blinded by the elegance of the view that linguistic cognition is just an extension of our overall cognition. Let's keep an open mind about there being a self-contained, domain-specific language network in the brain. From the busy field of neuroscience come a great many studies that fill out the details of our linguistic functions and how they relate to other high-level mental functions and to multi-purpose cognitive processes. Construction grammar will have to adapt to accommodate new findings about language and cognition.

### 5.2.2 The "Syntax-Lexicon Continuum"

All our linguistic knowledge can be described as essentially similar kinds of entities – symbolic units of form and function, called "constructions" in the theory – if it is agreed that syntax and lexicon, traditionally two rather different domains of analysis, form a continuum (e.g., among many further references, Fillmore, 1988: 42; Goldberg, 1995: 7; Jackendoff, 2008: 15; Hoffmann, 2013: 307). There are in fact two continua, which are orthogonal to each other (cf. Langacker, 2005a: 108): one of schematicity (Figure 8), the other of "size"/complexity (Figure 9).[18]

---

[18] Category labels in Figure 8 appear on the right of a lexical item or constituent. In Figure 3 and Figure 4, as well as in (4), they appeared on the left, on the inside of the opening bracket enclosing a constituent. There is absolutely no significance, however, to the positioning of syntactic labels.

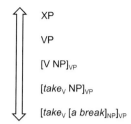

**Figure 8** Schematicity continuum, illustrated with phrasal units, in the middle of the "size"/complexity continuum (Figure 9). At the bottom, we find *take a break*, a lexically specific idiom. At the top, we find XP, where X is any part of speech that can head a phrase.

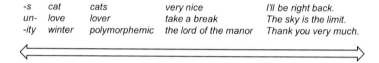

**Figure 9** "Size"/Complexity continuum, illustrated with some items at the bottom of the schematicity continuum (Figure 8), ranging from small/simple units (morphemes) to large/complex ones (sentences). Even further to the right we could find whole stretches of text, such as memorized nursery rhymes or lyrics of well-known songs.

For now, I will take no issue with the schematicity continuum, although the critical question is, of course, whether at the high end of the continuum, the abstract categories are still meaningful. Let us instead concentrate on the complexity continuum. This is problematic. First, it is doubtful whether bound morphemes as such have constructional status. We might want to embed them in schemas that also contains their base, such as $[N\text{-}s]_{N,\ plural}$ or $[un\text{-}A]_{A,\ neg}$, as is done in Construction Morphology (for introductions to constructionist approaches to morphology, see Booij, 2010, and Jackendoff & Audring, 2019). But that would mean, surprisingly, that the smallest meaningful units of language are actually located not at the leftmost end of the "size" continuum but only *somewhat* to the left, where we also find, in Figure 8, *cats*, *lover* and *polymorphemic*. And on the schematicity continuum, they would then also appear a little higher than these fully formed words.

A more important reason why the complexity continuum is problematic is that single words are quite different from combinations of words. Take compound nouns in English. On the one hand, one might argue that compounds are very similar to phrasal units. For instance, part of them (just like parts of phrases) can be replaced with *one*, as in (7a–c) (cf. also Goldberg & Michaelis, 2016, 236–237):[19]

(7)    a.  I very rarely saw him anywhere near drugs (apart from *prescription ones*). (COCA)

        b.  Lily must have noticed that Helen had taken winter clothes, not *summer ones*. (COCA)

        c.  I started working lunch shifts in addition to *dinner ones*. (COCA)

One might, furthermore, invoke the well-known possibility to have phrasal material inside compounds (e.g., [[ *foggy brain*]$_{N'}$ *syndrome*]$_N$) to further defend the position that words and phrases are similar: the latter can of course contain phrases (e.g. *Here's* [*a long noun phrase* [*with a prepositional phrase* [*with* [*inside that prepositional phrase*]$_{PP}$ *some extra prepositional phrases*]$_{PP}$]$_{PP}$]$_{NP}$), but so can, apparently, the former. On the other hand, one should realize that the possibility to include phrases inside words is heavily constrained. Cappelle (2022) notes that, for instance, cat biscuits suitable for fussy cats cannot simply be referred to by means of a phrasal compound:

(8)    ?*[[fussy cat]$_{N'}$ food]$_N$

The head of phrasal compounds tends to belong to a particular set of nouns, including *program*, *theory* and *system*.

Moreover, Shirtz & Goldberg (forthcoming) argue that when speakers use a phrase or clause formally as if it was a word, as in (9a–c), this comes with very special communicative intentions, involving the kind of wit and implied shared familiarity found also in observational comedy – especially if the event that is presumed to be recognizable and familiar is one that is not often talked about:

(9)    a.  a don't-mess-with-me driver

        b.  It's not a "call Ronan Farrow" scenario

        c.  We're at the people-are-moving-to-Jersey stage of nationwide collapse (examples from Shirtz & Goldberg, forthcoming)

The name that Shirtz and Goldberg (forthcoming) give to the construction, the "phrase-as-lemma construction," underscores the fact that (verb) phrases or

---

[19] This possibility seems rather constrained and unusual, however. What may partly sanction the example in (7a) is that *prescription drugs* is implicitly understood as contrasting with *recreational drugs*, a lexicalized phrasal combination. Furthermore, *prescription drugs* seems to be pronounced usually with primary stress on *drugs*, not on the stressed syllable of *prescription* (https://youglish.com/pronounce/prescription%20drugs/english?), so it may not be felt to be an ordinary compound. Likewise, *winter clothes* and *summer clothes* are also often pronounced with stress on *clothes*. Only (7c) is a fully legitimate example.

clauses do not *generally* find themselves in the same positions as words (inside a compound, say, or between a determiner and a noun).

The domain of words and the domain of word combinations – which grammatical theories, including CxG, refer to as morphology and syntax – are really quite different. Note, for instance, that it is hard to "manipulate" words (inflection aside). We cannot simply split them up, move any of their morphemes around, and so on. Ordering alternations of the kind we know from syntax do not seem to exist in the domain of morphology. In short, words are much more "solid" than phrasal or clausal units. In light of words' distinctively cohesive nature, it seems best to acknowledge that there is a (perhaps still somewhat permeable) boundary between morphological constructions and syntactic ones.

This is supported by neuroscientific findings involving a certain brain response, the mismatch negativity (MMN). Neuroimaging can pick up a spike in brainwaves when we hear sounds or syllables completing actual words, but a reduction of brain activity triggered by words in common phrasal or clausal combinations (see Pulvermüller, Cappelle, & Shtyrov, 2013, for some discussion and references). Apparently, our cognition treats words in a fundamentally different way from combinations of words. This is something that CxGians should be prepared to accept. If they do, it will not bring about any significant changes to their daily research. It is just the CxG "background story" that will sound a little different.

### 5.2.3 Isomorphism

The claim that knowledge of language fully consists of meaningful, symbolic units is also protected, in a way, by the (often implicit) idea that for each form, there's just one meaning being expressed, and, vice versa, for one meaning, just one form encoding it. Such "isomorphism" ensures that we can easily think of the constructi-con as a structured network of Saussurean signs.

In line with this, Goldberg (1995: 67) claims that when two constructions differ in form, they should also differ in their semantics, or if not in their semantics, then in their pragmatics (cf. also the second tenet (left) in Figure 1). This principle of no synonymy has recently been challenged (e.g., Uhrig, 2015; Laporte, Larsson, & Goulart, 2021). Leclercq and Morin (2023) critically review purported theory-internal problems with this principle, as well as apparent evidence against it. They propose to rebrand it as "the principle of no equivalence" and to include possible *social* differences among constructions with identical semantics and pragmatics. This saves the principle of no synonymy/equivalence and the core idea of CxG can thus preserve its plausibility.

I suspect criticism of isomorphism will keep cropping up, however, especially from diachronic linguists (e.g., Van de Velde, 2014). In the history of a language, different forms can come to have overlapping functions and even become ever more similar to each other, but functionally similar forms can also go their separate ways again, influenced by the bigger constructional families each form belongs to (De Smet et al., 2018).

Isomorphism is not crucial for CxG to survive: there can be many-to-many mappings in the constructi-con. What would be worse, however, would be "mappings" where some forms have no associated meaning. This leads us to the next section, where we attempt to find a way to disprove CxG's boldest claim.

### 5.3 Formulate a Crucial Test

What's interesting in Leclercq's quote in Section 5.1 is the hedge in the statement that linguistic knowledge consists "only (or mostly)" of knowledge of constructions. With this parenthetical qualification, there is some deviation from the well-known bolder statement that "[w]hat makes a theory that allows for constructions a 'construction-based' theory is . . . the idea that the network of constructions captures our knowledge of language *in toto* – in other words, it's constructions all the way down" (Goldberg, 2003: 223). Leclercq's description of CxG suggests that it is possible to not be fully committal about whether or not all of knowledge about language is constructional and still formulate the essence of the theory.

Traugott (2022), however, takes up the challenge to find forms not associated with function, as a crucial test for CxG. The different positions of discourse markers in a clause are construction candidates. Since *after all* in modern English can have a justification function in pre-clausal, medial and post-clausal position (e.g., [*We shouldn't be too harsh on ourselves.*] {*After all*} we're {*after all*} only human {*after all*}), Traugott concludes that position *doesn't* qualify as a construction (as per the principle of no synonymy mentioned in Section 5.2.2). "Therefore, it's NOT 'constructions all the way down' (Goldberg 2003: 223)!" (Traugott, 2022: 179).

One could disagree with the middle step in Traugott's reasoning – that because the same meaning can be conveyed by two or three alternatives, these can't be different constructions. After all, the exact distribution of functions (concession, justification, etc.) is still different for the three positions. (To express justification, for instance, *after all* is not often used clause-finally: try moving it in the preceding sentence.) Nevertheless, a point that *could* be made is that speakers of a language apparently know where certain elements can be put and that this knowledge pertains primarily to something formal, not to something functional.

### 5.3.1 Rationale for a Crucial Test

Construction Grammar, embraced most strictly, predicts that there are no bits of knowledge which we would like to call constructional (in the sense of relating to patterns) but which are devoid of meaning or function (with these latter terms understood even in a broad sense). The set-up for a crucial test for CxG grammar can therefore be formulated as in (10):

(10)     Commonly observed structural regularities in a language must either be shown to be associated with meaning or function, or be shown not to be known by the speakers of that language.

The idea is that we should look for patterns that seem to have no semantic or other functional correlate. If we indeed cannot think of any function – something that should be agreed on widely among CxGians – then we should find out whether speakers are aware of that functionless formal regularity. Construction Grammar predicts that speakers should not have any knowledge of it. If it then turned out that they do, we would have evidence that CxG makes a false prediction – not just a harmless false prediction, but one that would reveal that CxG is not correct in its most radical, boldest claim.

Of course, our success of operationalizing this depends on our ability to agree on what we, as linguists, take *meaning* or *function* to mean (Hartmann, 2015). It also depends on how we could measure knowledge of a pattern. As mentioned in Section 3.1, Ziegler and colleagues' (2019) experiment showed that the use of the English passive construction is not primed by intransitive locative sentences with the same syntactic structure ([NP Aux V PP]). Interestingly, their experiment does make use of the concept of "abstract, content-less tree structure," the premise being that the passive and the stimuli sentences have a common constituent structure. But here's the crux: can it really be shown that speakers of English have not integrated this structure into their knowledge of English grammar? If it could be demonstrated that speakers *do* know about this meaningless pattern (that is, that all they know about it is that it is a valid sequence of slots to be filled), then we would have shown wrong the basic claim of CxG.

### 5.3.2 What Could Be Truly Meaningless Syntactic Patterns? The Transitive? Gapping?

Hilpert (2019, 62–68) provides an interesting discussion about the question of whether there are any truly meaningless constructions. Does a sentence such as *Bob heard a noise* instantiate an argument-structure construction on a par with, for instance, the ditransitive or the resultative construction? But what would be the meaning of such a general transitive construction? "The stereotypical transitive verb," Jackendoff (2002: 135) writes, "has an Agent acting on Patient." Examples that come to mind are *eat*, *hit* or *throw*. It might indeed be possible to describe the transitive construction as having a prototypical meaning, with a doer performing an action on an undergoer. However, Jackendoff (2002: 135–136) quickly goes on to add that the transitive pattern occurs with various other thematic roles. His examples include *John imagined/mentioned his pet elephant*, Emily *likes/fears/despises cats*, *Liana left/entered the room*, *The meeting lasted seven hours*, *The book weighs three pounds* and *The doctor underwent an operation*, among others. This makes it almost fruitless to characterize the transitive pattern in semantic terms.

Langacker (2002: 221) does just that, however, and perceives there to be an "asymmetrical relationship" in both prototypical actions and in cases like *Several witnesses saw the accident* and *I have carefully considered your offer*, where a sentient being creates a mental representation of a nonphysical entity and in doing so, moves, as it were, into contact with it, something which costs mental energy. Only as a limiting case, when neither participant is truly energetic, does the speaker have to simply pick out an entity as the relational figure (realized as the subject in an active clause). There is objectively speaking no inherent asymmetry in a situation that can be described by both *The fifth floor contains a library* and *A library occupies the fifth floor*. In picking one participant to be the subject, the speaker then subjectively imposes some asymmetry on the extralinguistic situation. Legallois (2022), too, provides a semantic analysis of the transititive construction, not in terms of a prototypical core or a single highly abstract schematic meaning like asymmetry, but by identifying several "archetypical," so-called "localist" relations that link the participants: in various domains (physical, emotional, social), the object entity may be brought closer to or moved away from the subject entity, or be included in the latter's sphere.

One syntactic phenomenon which Hilpert marks out as a true challenge to CxG's bold claim is ellipsis. Consider the sentence in (11):

(11)    One sock lay on the sofa, the other under it.
        (Hilpert, 2019: 62)

This sentence exhibits so-called "gapping": between the constituents *the other* and *under it* in the second conjunct, there is an empty position (a "gap") that could also have been filled by a verb, the same verb as in the first conjunct:

(12)     One sock lay on the sofa, the other lay under it.

Fillmore and colleagues (2012: 326–327) mention the omission of the verb in a sentence like (11) as one of several cases they discuss "for which it is unnecessary to associate meanings with syntactic structures" (p. 326). While Hilpert shows how the other cases Fillmore and colleagues (2012) mention can be tackled with a prototype analysis, a schematic analysis or a combination of these and thus, "with a little goodwill … be brought into the fold of the construct-i-con" (p. 67), he admits that elliptical constructions would have to be assigned a high score for "meaninglessness."

It may be premature, however, to give up all attempts at associating a semantic or functional content with gapping. (For constructionist treatments of gapping and other forms of ellipsis, see Culicover & Jackendoff, 2005: 233–300; Goldberg & Perek, 2019; for gapping in particular, see Bîlbîie & de la Fuente, 2019.) Note that gapping occurs in (syndetic or, as in (11), asyndetic) coordination. Coordination, which is a natural environment for elliptical phenomena, often has the effect of grouping disparate elements together and presenting them as single units. Consider the following sentence:

(13)     My wife and I were happy for twenty years. Then we met.
         (Rodney Dangerfield)

The coordinated sequence *my wife and I* of course gets the hearer on the wrong foot: it creates the expectation that the sentence is a single statement about the speaker and their spouse as a married couple, but then it turns out that there are two propositions at stake (one about the speaker's wife's happy twenty-years-long life before meeting and eventually marrying the speaker and another about the speaker's equally long happy life before meeting and marrying her). Consider, conversely, the following line from a famous movie:

(14)     Maybe it's "Barbie," and it's "Ken."

Here, Barbie, the protagonist of the eponymous motion picture, reacts to an existential crisis of the main male antagonist, who had previously told her, "I don't know who I am without you … It's 'Barbie and Ken.'" By undoing the coordination in this NP and using two coordinated main clauses instead, the speaker in (14) wants to convince the listener that they are two separate entities, neither being an accessory to the other.

What this implies for gapping is that, due to an explicit second verb being absent, the two paired entities involved in the two conjoined clauses are construed much more as making up a single, complex item – like *my wife and I* and like *Barbie and Ken* – than when there is a verb in each conjunct. Note that

(11) is more likely to be uttered than (12) in response to a question like "Where were his socks?" By contrast, (12) would probably be more appropriate as an answer to the question what an entire room looked like, and it could then be preceded and/or followed by other separate propositions, for example, "Discarded wrappers covered the floor, one sock lay on the sofa, the other lay under it, and half-empty beer bottles were scattered across the coffee table."

In short, gapping and other elliptical phenomena might not be suitable candidates to use in a crucial test after all. It will therefore not be easy to find structural patterns that the community of CxGians can all agree on are not associated with some kind of meaning.

### 5.3.3 Might Constructed Constructions Be a Solution?

Speakers surely realize that (15a–b) exhibit acceptable structures while (16a–b) do not, even in the absence of knowledge of the major lexical items involved. (As in Johnson & Goldberg's (2012) study with "Jabberwocky sentences," the use of nonsense words ensures that what is tested is knowledge of schemas that are as abstract as possible.)

(15)  a.  The brap was jorped by the molp.
      b.  The kiff was tamming near the norps.

(16)  a.  *The brap was by the molp jorped.
      b.  *The kiff was near the norps tamming.

The difference in acceptability between (15a–b) and (16a–b) could actually be tested experimentally, of course, but the outcome would likely confirm that speakers of English simply *know* that the main verb should appear before a PP, not after it. One might object that all that speakers of English have to know here is the word order of the passive and that of the locative – constructions which *are* themselves meaningful. It thus remains hard to test whether language users have knowledge of something formal that is not tied to anything semantic. But note that the verb-final position is excluded in a wide range of patterns. If it is the case that a mother schema naturally emerges from a large number of types, the examples in (17a–f) strongly suggest that speakers of English have internalized a general, abstract "rule" (i.e., a syntactic schema) that requires the main verb to appear before and not after its complements. Compare (17a–e) and (18a–e):

(17)  a.  The druff has been blopping the swugs.
      b.  The plam has snoused her the druke.
      c.  The snaff was flurking its way into the thomp.
      d.  The splink has chossed it miggy.
      e.  The criff has tashed the blop right into the fress.

(18)    a.  *The druff has been the swugs blopping.
        b.  *The plam has her the druke snoused.
        c.  *The snaff was its way into the thomp flurking.
        d.  *The splink has it miggy chossed.
        e.  *The criff has the blop right into the fress tashed.

Now, to exclude the possibility that test subjects in an (as of yet) imaginary syntactic judgment experiment *still* rely on known meaningful patterns to rate the sentences in (18a–e) as seriously degraded, one could consider *inventing* sentence patterns, which either respect or violate the main-verb-before-complement(s) rule ((19a–c) vs. (20a–c)) or another structural requirement, such as the presumed rule that clauses should follow PPs ((19d) vs. (20d)) or that a post-verbal "ethical dative" pronoun should precede any other post-verbal constituent ((19e) vs. (20e)):

(19)    a.  *There plommifies a zope the glaf.
        b.  *The grat was freeping her the troaf some prash.
        c.  *The broaf has clermized onto gruning them.
        d.  *It was snarfy of you that you could splongle.
        e.  *It was him really zonky to frabber this again.

(20)    a.  *There a zope the glaf plommifies.
        b.  *The grat was her the troaf some prash greeping.
        c.  *The broaf has onto gruning them clermized.
        d.  *It was snarfy that you could splongle of you.
        e.  *It was really zonky to frabber this again him.

The invented structures used in (19a–e) lack any instantiations and it would therefore be difficult to argue that they can be associated with a conventional meaning. Some might not even evoke any interpretable scene at all. If it turned out that test subjects in a rating or forced-choice experiment were nonetheless fairly consistent in judging the sentences in (19a–e) as a little *less* unacceptable than, or preferable to, those in (20a–e), this would mean that the central claim of CxG is falsified. Indeed, it would mean that language users have access to knowledge about their language that is purely structural (e.g., "in VPs, the main verb appears before any complements"). *Ergo*, regardless of the outcome of such an experiment, it could then be concluded that CxG is a falsifiable theory. It thus would appear that there is an imaginable way of testing that not all of a speaker's knowledge of a language consists of form-function pairings.

Some caveats are in order. First, even though these sentences are nonexistent (in English), test participants may still interpret them as meaningful. This is likely the case for (19d), which uses a *that*-clause where a *to*-infinitive constituent would be grammatical. In fact, a *that*-clause is perhaps not fully unacceptable, which is a further complication. If an "invented" sentence type can be made sense of because it bears a very close formal resemblance to, or alternates with, an existing sentence pattern, it would of course not be suitable for a crucial experiment. Second, some of the patterns in (19a–e) may exist in other languages. One would therefore have to make sure that the test participants do not speak any language that licenses these patterns, or at least, one would have to check their knowledge of other languages than English and find out whether their judgments are influenced by them. Third, participants may find a sentence from the set in (19a–e) more acceptable than the corresponding sentence in (20a–e) because, even though the full sentence is ungrammatical, most of it is. For instance, before the appearance of the final post-verbal NP, (19a) and (19b) seem perfectly fine.[20]

In any case, note that in order to produce a valid nonsense word, we also have to rely on some purely formal (namely phonotactic) knowledge of the language. We know that *brap* at least *could* be an ordinary English word, unlike *bnap* or *mbap*, but there is nothing semantic, pragmatic or otherwise functional involved in this certainty. On the basis of this and quite a few other such kinds of nonsymbolic knowledge, the parallel architecture (PA) and its component relational morphology (RM), a "cousin" of CxG, extend the scope of constructions:

> The PA, like CxG and unlike traditional generative grammar (including the minimalist program), argues that the grammar must include constructions that specifically link syntactic form to meaning, such as the *way*-construction (e.g., *Harry hiccupped his miserable way down the hall*). But it admits the possibility of schemas/constructions that do not involve semantics, for instance phrase structure rules, phonotactics, meaningless morphological elements such as linking elements in compounds, and grammatical "glue" such as *do*-support and the *of* in *picture of Bill*. RM further extends the use of schemas to phenomena where meaning plays no role, such as the relation of phonology to orthography and the relation of poetic texts to a metrical grid (Jackendoff and Audring, [2019], ch. 8). Hence the PA views constructions that relate form and function as only a subset of a speaker's full knowledge of language. (Jackendoff & Audring, 2020: 2)

---

[20] In this respect, these sentences are somewhat similar to so-called "Escher sentences." However, the latter seem, at first pass, fine as a whole, from beginning to end:

(i)  a.   More people have been to Russia than I have.
          (Montalbetti, 1984: 6)
     b.   More people drink Guinness than I do.
          (Hurford, 2012: 214)

These are "syntactic illusions." Superficially, they sound fully acceptable and you may not notice there is anything wrong with them until you realize that they are, in fact, not coherent at all.

One may disagree with certain points, for instance with the meaninglessness of *of*. But the message should be clear: if we care for CxG, we shouldn't shy away from acknowledging kinds of non-symbolic knowledge.

## 6 Keep Calm and Constructi-con

> But I have always stressed the need of some dogmatism: the dogmatic scientist has an important role to play. If we give in to criticism too easily, we shall never find out where the real power of our theories lies.
>
> (Popper, 1970: 55)

So, what if our knowledge of language includes knowledge of meaningless structures? What if certain aspects of language processing turn out not to tap into domain-general cognitive functions? Indeed, so what? The coming to light of these and other facts running counter to CxG dogma does not have to bring about the downfall of this theory.

In contrast to the currently prevailing form of CxG, PA and RM, mentioned at the end of Section 5, accept semantically empty constructions and, more as "a philosophical point of divergence," domain-specific aspects of language. I agree with Ray Jackendoff and Jenny Audring when they add:

> We believe that these points of difference can easily be grafted onto more standard versions of CxG, as what RJ's colleague Dan Dennett calls "friendly amendments." (Jackendoff & Audring, 2020: 2)

Admitting functionally void schemas, whether or not we want to still consider them constructions, does not seriously jeopardize the theory if they are seen as an extreme phenomenon at the upper end of the schematicity continuum. Accepting some degree of syntactic autonomy is therefore not a "crime," as Langacker (2008: 168) calls this, maybe not even fully ironically. Traugott (2022) is right when she writes:

> I don't think the fact that Goldberg overstated the ubiquity of constructions in the grammar in any way counters the value of Construction Grammar. . . . It's possible that it would be good to adopt weaker statements than Goldberg's, but then we would not be prompted to think so carefully. I think it is good that she said: "It's constructions all the way down," because that has challenged us to think about exactly where constructions occur and what the constraints on understanding them are. (Traugott, 2022: 179)

The notion of constructions as a heuristic tool (cf. Hartmann & Pleyer, 2021: 2) invites us to at least *wonder* about the potential meaningfulness of abstract patterns. Likewise, even if we're not yet fully aware of all the complex workings of the brain and mind, recognizing the relevance of certain general cognitive capacities, such as our ability to abstract away over similar individual experiences, has yielded valuable linguistic analyses, and still does.

That CxG is falsifiable is good news; that it quite likely will be or already has been falsified perhaps less so. But let's not forget that CxG is not just a theory but a veritable program, and a scientific, still progressive one at that, as Lakatos (1978) would have perceived it. The theory may be somewhat wrong, but we are clearly doing something right.

# References

Anthonissen, L. & Petré, P. (2019). Grammaticalization and the linguistic individual: New avenues in lifespan research. *Linguistics Vanguard*, 5(s2). http://doi.org/10.1515/lingvan-2018-0037.

Audring, J. (2019). Mothers or sisters? The encoding of morphological knowledge. *Word Structure*, 12(3), 274–296.

Barðdal, J. (2011). The rise of Dative Substitution in the history of Icelandic: A diachronic construction grammar account, *Lingua*, 121, 60–79.

Barðdal, J., Smirnova, E., Sommerer, L. & Gildea, S., eds. (2015). *Diachronic Construction Grammar*. Amsterdam: John Benjamins.

Berwick, R. C. & Chomsky, N. (2016). *Why Only Us: Language and Evolution*. Cambridge, MA: MIT Press.

Bîlbîie, G. & de la Fuente, I. (2019). Can gapping be embedded? Experimental evidence from Spanish. *Glossa: A Journal of General Linguistics*, 4(1), 110. http://doi.org/10.5334/gjgl.782.

Bird, A. (2018). Thomas Kuhn. In E. N. Zalta, U. Nodelman, C. Allen, et al., eds., *Stanford Encyclopedia of Philosophy*. https://plato.stanford.edu/entries/thomas-kuhn/.

Blank, I. & Fedorenko, E. (2017). Domain-general brain regions do not track linguistic input as closely as language-selective regions. *Journal of Neuroscience*, 37(41), 9999–10011. http://doi.org/10.1523/JNEUROSCI.3642-16.2017.

Boas, H. C. (2003). *A Constructional Approach to Resultatives*. Standard, CA: CSLI Publications.

Boas, H. C. (2008). Determining the structure of lexical entries and grammatical constructions in Construction Grammar. *Annual Review of Cognitive Linguistics*, 6(1), 113–144.

Boas, H. C. (2021). Construction Grammar and frame semantics. In W. Xu & J. R. Taylor, eds., *The Routledge Handbook of Cognitive Linguistics*. New York: Routledge, pp. 43–77.

Boas, H. C., ed. (2022). *Directions for Pedagogical Construction Grammar*. Berlin: De Gruyter Mouton.

Boas, H. C., Leino, J., & Lyngfelt, B. (to appear a). Berkeley, we have a problem: Some questions for Construction Grammar. *Constructions and Frames*.

Boas, H. C., Leino, J., & Lyngfelt, B. (to appear b). Introduction: Issues of the theme. *Construction and Frames*.

Booij, G. (2010). *Construction Morphology*. Oxford: Oxford University Press.

Bouveret, M. & Legallois, D. (2012). Cognitive linguistics and the notion of construction in French studies: An overview. In D. Legallois & M. Bouveret, eds., *Constructions in French*. Amsterdam: John Benjamins.

Branigan, H. P., Pickering, M. J., Liversedge, S. P., Stewart, A. J., & Urbach, T. P. (1995). Syntactic priming: Investigating the mental representation of language. *Journal of Psycholinguistic Research*, 24, 489–506.

Broccias, C. (2013). Cognitive Grammar. In T. Hoffmann & G. Trousdale, eds., *The Oxford Handbook of Construction Grammar*. New York: Oxford University Press, pp. 191–210.

Butler, C. S. & Gonzálvez-García, F. (2014). *Exploring Functional-Cognitive Space*. Amsterdam: John Benjamins.

Bybee, J. (2010). *Language, Usage and Cognition*. Cambridge: Cambridge University Press.

Bybee, J. (2012). Domain-general processes as the basis for grammar. In M. Tallerman & K. R. Gibson, eds., *The Oxford Handbook of Language Evolution*, Oxford: Oxford University Press, pp. 528–536.

Bybee, J. (2013). Usage-based theory and exemplar representations of constructions. In T. Hoffmann & G. Trousdale, eds., *The Oxford Handbook of Construction Grammar*. Oxford: Oxford University Press, pp. 49–69.

Campbell, K. L. & Tyler, L. K. (2018). Language-related domain-specific and domain-general systems in the human brain. *Current Opinion in Behavioral Sciences*, 21, 132–137.

Cappelle, B. (2002). And up it rises: Particle preposing in English. In N. Dehé, R. Jackendoff, A. McIntyre & S. Urban, eds., *Verb-Particle Explorations*. Berlin: Mouton de Gruyter, pp. 43–66.

Cappelle, B. (2006). Particle placement and the case for "allostructions." *Constructions*, special volume 1, 1–28. https://constructions.journals.hhu.de/article/view/381.

Cappelle, B. (2008). The grammar of complex particle phrases in English. In A. Asbury, J. Dotlacil, B. Gehrke, & R. Nouwen, eds., *Syntax and Semantics of Spatial P*. Amsterdam: John Benjamins, pp. 103–145.

Cappelle, B. (2009). Contextual cues for particle placement: Multiplicity, motivation, modeling. In A. Bergs & G. Diewald, eds., *Context in Construction Grammar*. Amsterdam: John Benjamins, pp. 145–192.

Cappelle, B. (2022). Lexical integrity: A mere contruct or more a construction? *Yearbook of the German Cognitive Linguistics Association (GCLA)*, 10, 183–216.

Cappelle, B. (2023). Verb-particle constructions. In M. Aronoff, ed., *Oxford Bibliographies in Linguistics*. New York: Oxford University Press. http://doi.org/10.1093/OBO/9780199772810-0311.

Cappelle, B., Fagundes Travassos, P., Almeida Mota, N., et al. (2021). Constructional variation: Unveiling aspects of linguistic knowledge: Interview with Bert Cappelle. *Revista da Anpoll*, 52(Special Issue), 258–306.

Cappelle, B. & Grabar, N. (2016). Towards an n-grammar of English. In S. De Knop & G. Gilquin, eds., *Applied Construction Grammar*. Berlin: De Gruyter Mouton, pp. 271–302.

Chomsky, N. (1957). *Syntactic Structures*. The Hague: Mouton.

Chomsky, N. (1961). On the notion "rule of grammar." In R. Jacobson, ed., *Structure of Language and Its Mathematical Aspects*. Providence, RI: American Mathematical Society, pp. 6–24.

Chomsky, N. (1962). Explanatory models in linguistics. In E. Nagel, P. Suppes, & A. Tarski, eds., *Logic, Methodology and Philosophy of Science*. Stanford, CA: Stanford University Press, pp. 528–550.

Chomsky, N. (1964). *Current Issues in Linguistic Theory*. The Hague: Mouton.

Chomsky, N. (1965). *Aspects of the Theory of Syntax*. Cambridge, MA: MIT Press.

Chomsky, N. (1981). *Lectures on Government and Binding*. Dordrecht: Foris Publications.

Chomsky, N. (2000). Minimalist inquiries: The framework. In R. Martin, D. Michaels, & J. Uriagereka, eds., *Step by Step: Essays on Minimalist Syntax in Honor of Howard Lasnik*. Cambridge, MA: MIT Press, pp. 89–155.

Chomsky, N. (2005). Three factors in language design. *Linguistic Inquiry*, 36(1), 1–22.

Chomsky, N. (2007). Of minds and language. *Biolinguistics*, 1, 9–27.

Chomsky, N. (2015[1995]). *The Minimalist Program*, twentieth-anniversary edition. Cambridge, MA: MIT Press.

Chomsky, N. (2017). Language architecture and its import for evolution. *Neuroscience and Biobehavioral Reviews*, 81(B), 295–300.

Christiansen, M. H. & Chater, N. (2008). Language as shaped by the brain. *Behavioral and Brain Sciences*, 31(5), 489–509.

Clark, A. & Lappin, S. (2011). *Linguistic Nativism and the Poverty of the Stimulus*. Malden, MA: Wiley-Blackwell.

Crain, S., Koring, L., & Thornton, R. (2017). Language acquisition from a biolinguistic perspective. *Neuroscience & Biobehavioral Reviews*, 81(B), 120–149.

Culicover, P. W. & Jackendoff, R. (2005). *Simpler Syntax*. New York: Oxford University Press.

Dąbrowska, E. (2015). What exactly is universal grammar, and has anyone seen it? *Frontiers in Psychology*, 6 (Article 852). http://doi.org/10.3389/fpsyg.2015.00852.

Dąbrowska, E. & Divjak, D., eds. (2015). *Handbook of Cognitive Linguistics*. Berlin: Walter de Gruyter.

Dancygier, B., ed. (2021). *The Cambridge Handbook of Cognitive Linguistics*. Cambridge: Cambridge University Press.

Davies, M. (2008–19). *The Corpus of Contemporary American English: 600 million words*, *1990–present*. http://corpus.byu.edu/coca/.

De Knop, S. & Gilquin, G., eds. (2016). *Applied Construction Grammar*. Berlin: De Gruyter Mouton.

Derksen, M. (2019). Putting Popper to work. *Theory & Psychology*, 29(4), 449–465.

Desagulier, G. (2017). *Corpus Linguistics and Statistics with R: Introduction to Quantitative Methods in Linguistics*. New York: Springer.

Diachek, E., Blank, I., Siegelman, M., Affourtit, J., & Fedorenko, E. (2020). The domain-general multiple-demand (MD) network does not support core aspects of language comprehension: A large-scale fMRI investigation. *Journal of Neuroscience*, 40(23), 4536–4550.

Diessel, H. (2023). *The Constructicon: Taxonomies and Networks*. Cambridge: Cambridge University Press.

Dingemanse, M. (2007). We need simpler syntax, but we can do without a grammar of the gaps. https://ideophone.org/simpler-syntax-or-grammar-of-the-gaps/.

Divjak, D. (2015). Four challenges for usage-based linguistics. In J. Daems, E. Zenner, K. Heylen, D. Speelman, & H. Cuyckens, eds., *Change of Paradigms: New Paradoxes: Recontextualizing Language and Linguistics*. Berlin: Walter de Gruyter, pp. 297–309.

Dunn, J. (2017a). Computational learning of construction grammars. *Language and Cognition*, 9(2), 254–292.

Dunn, J. (2017b). Learnability and falsifiability of Construction Grammars. *Proceedings of the Linguistic Society of America*, 2(1), 1–15.

Earp, B. & Trafimow, D. (2015). Replication, falsification, and the crisis of confidence in social psychology. *Frontiers in Psychology*, 6 (Article 621). http://doi.org/10.3389/fpsyg.2015.00621.

Edmonds, D. & Warburton, N. (2010). *Philosophy Bites*. New York: Oxford University Press.

Evans, N. & Levinson, S. C. (2009a). The myth of language universals: Language diversity and its importance for cognitive science. *Behavioral and Brain Sciences*, 32(5), 429–448.

Evans, N. & Levinson, S. C. (2009b). With diversity in mind: Freeing the language sciences from universal grammar. *Behavioral and Brain Sciences*, 32(5), 472–484.

Evans, V. & Green, M. (2002). *Cognitive Linguistics: An Introduction.* Edinburgh: Edinburgh University Press.

Everett, D. L. (2005). Cultural constraints on grammar and cognition in Pirahã. *Current Anthropology*, 46(4), 621–646.

Fedorenko, E., Behr, M. K., & Kanwisher, N. (2011). Functional specificity for high-level linguistic processing in the human brain. *Proceedings of the National Academy of Sciences*, 108(39), 16428–16433.

Fedorenko, E., Blank, I. A., Siegelman, M., and Mineroff, Z. (2020). Lack of selectivity for syntax relative to word meanings throughout the language network. *Cognition*, 203 (Article 104348). http://doi.org/10.1016/j.cognition .2020.104348.

Fedorenko, E. & Thompson-Schill, S. L. (2014). Reworking the language network. *Trends in Cognitive Sciences*, 18(3), 120–126. http://doi.org/ 10.1016/j.tics.2013.12.006.

Feyerabend, P. K. (1975). *Against Method: Outline of an Anarchistic Theory of Knowledge.* London: New Left Books.

Fillmore, C. J. (1982). Frame semantics. In the Linguistic Society of Korea, ed. *Linguistics in the Morning Calm.* Seoul: Hanshin, pp. 111–137.

Fillmore, C. J. (1985a). Frames and the semantics of understanding. *Quaderni di Semantica*, 6(2), 222–254.

Fillmore, C. J. (1985b). Syntactic intrusions and the notion of grammatical construction. In M. Niepokuj, M. van Clay, V. Nikiforidou, & D. Feder, eds., *Proceedings of the Eleventh Annual Meeting of the Berkeley Linguistic Society.* Berkeley, CA: Berkeley Linguistic Society, pp. 73–86.

Fillmore, C. J. (1988). The mechanisms of "Construction Grammar." In S. Axmaker, A. Jaisser, & H. Singmaster, eds., *Proceedings of the Fourteenth Annual Meeting of the Berkeley Linguistics Society*, Berkeley, CA: Berkeley Linguistic Society, pp. 35–55.

Fillmore, C. J. (1989). Grammatical construction theory and the familiar dichotomies. In R. Dietrich & C. F. Graumann, eds., *Language Processing in Social Context.* Amsterdam: North-Holland/Elsevier, pp. 17–38.

Fillmore, C. J. (2020). *Papers on Linguistic Theory and Constructions.* Vol. III of Form and Meaning in Language, edited by P. Gras, J.-O. Östman, & J. Verschueren. Stanford, CA: CSLI Publications.

Fillmore, C. J., Kay, P., & O'Connor, C. (1988). Regularity and idiomaticity in grammatical constructions: The case of *let alone. Language*, 64(3), 501–538.

Fillmore, C. J., Lee-Goldman, R. R., & Rhomieux, R. (2012). The FrameNet Constructicon. In H. C. Boas & I. A. Sag (eds.), *Sign-based Construction Grammar.* Stanford, CA: CSLI Publications, pp. 309–372.

Forsberg, M., Johansson, R., Bäckström, L., et al. (2014). From construction candidates to construction entries: An experiment using semi-automatic methods for identifying constructions in corpora. *Constructions and Frames*, 6(1), 114–135.

Geeraarts, D. & Cuyckens, H., eds. (2007). *The Oxford Handbook of Cognitive Linguistics*. Oxford: Oxford University Press.

Gisborne, N. (2011). Constructions, word grammar, and grammaticalization. *Cognitive Linguistics*, 22(1), 155–182. http://doi.org/10.1515/cogl.2011.007.

Goldberg, A. E. (1995). *Constructions: A Construction Grammar Approach to Argument Structure*. Chicago, IL: University of Chicago Press.

Goldberg, A. E. (1996). Jackendoff and construction-based grammar. *Cognitive Linguistics*, 7(1), 3–19.

Goldberg, A. E. (2003). Constructions: A new theoretical approach to language. *Trends in Cognitive Sciences*, 7(5), 219–224.

Goldberg, A. E. (2006). *Constructions at Work: The Nature of Generalization in Language*. New York: Oxford University Press.

Goldberg, A. E. (2013). Constructionist approaches. In T. Hoffman and G. Trousdale, eds., *The Oxford Handbook of Construction Grammar*. New York: Oxford University Press, pp. 15–31.

Goldberg, A. E. & Michaelis, L. A. (2016). One among many: Anaphoric *one* and its relationship with numeral *one*. *Cognitive Science*, 41(Suppl. 2), 233–258.

Goldberg, A. E. & Perek, F. (2019). Ellipsis in Construction Grammar. In J. van Craenenbroeck & T. Temmerman, eds., *The Oxford Handbook of Ellipsis*. Oxford: Oxford University Press, pp. 188–204.

Gries, S. T. & Stefanowitsch, A. (2004). Extending collostructional analysis: A corpus-based perspective on "alternations." *International Journal of Corpus Linguistics*, 9(1), 97–129.

Halliday, M. A. K. (2003[1964]). Syntax and the consumer. In J. J. Webster, ed., *On Language and Linguistics*. Vol. 3 in the Collected Works of M. A. K. Halliday. London: Continuum, pp. 36–49.

Halliday, M. A. K. & Matthiessen, C. M. I. M. (2013). *Halliday's Introduction to Functional Grammar*, 4th ed. London: Routledge.

Harris, R. A. (2021). *The Linguistics Wars: Chomsky, Lakoff, and the Battle over Deep Structure*, 2nd ed. New York: Oxford University Press.

Hartmann, S. (2015). Empty constructions and the meaning of "meaning." *Replicated Typo*. www.replicatedtypo.com/empty-constructions-and-the-meaning-of-meaning/10316.html

Hartmann S. & Pleyer, M. (2021). Constructing a protolanguage: Reconstructing prehistoric languages in a usage-based construction grammar framework.

*Philosophical Transactions of the Royal Society B*, 376(1824). http://doi.org/10.1098/rstb.2020.0200.

Hartmann, S. & Sommerer, L. (2022). "Constructions": Entering a new era. *Constructions*, 14, 1–3.

Haspelmath, M. (2020). Human linguisticality and the building blocks of languages. *Frontiers in Psychology*, 31 (Article 3389). http://doi.org/10.3389/fpsyg.2019.03056.

Haspelmath, M. (2023). On what a construction is. *Constructions*, 15(1). http://doi.org/10.24338/cons-539.

Hauser, M. D., Chomsky, N., & Fitch, W. T. (2002). The faculty of language: What is it, who has it, and how did it evolve? *Science*, 298, 1569–1579.

Hendrikx, L. & Van Goethem, K. (2018). Intensifying constructions in second language acquisition: A diasystematic-constructionist approach. In H. C. Boas & S. Höder, eds., *Constructions in Contact 2: Language Change, Multilingual Practices, and Additional Language Acquisition*. Amsterdam: John Benjamins.

Herbst, T. (2016). Foreign language learning is construction learning – what else? Moving towards Pedagogical Construction Grammar. In S. De Knop & G. Gilquin, eds., *Applied Construction Grammar*. Berlin: De Gruyter Mouton, pp. 21–52.

Hilpert, M. (2019). *Construction Grammar and Its Application to English*, 2nd ed. Edinburgh: Edinburgh University Press.

Hilpert, M. (2021). *Ten Lectures on Diachronic Construction Grammar*. Leiden: Brill Online.

Höder, S. (2012). Multilingual constructions: A diasystematic approach to common structures. In K. Braunmüller & C. Gabriel, eds., *Multilingual Individuals and Multilingual Societies*. Amsterdam: John Benjamins, pp. 241–257.

Höder, S. (2019). Phonological schematicity in multilingual constructions: A diasystematic perspective on lexical form. *Word Structure*, 12(3), 334–352.

Hoffmann, T. (2013). Abstract phrasal and clausal constructions. In T. Hoffmann & G. Trousdale, eds., *The Oxford Handbook of Construction Grammar*. New York: Oxford University Press, pp. 307–328.

Hoffmann, T. (2020). What would it take for us to abandon Construction Grammar: Falsifiability, confirmation bias and the future of the constructionist enterprise. *Belgian Journal of Linguistics*, 34, 149–161.

Hoffmann, T. (2022). *Construction Grammar: The Structure of English*. Cambridge: Cambridge University Press.

Hoffmann, T. & Trousdale, G., eds. (2013). *The Oxford Handbook of Construction Grammar*. New York: Oxford University Press.

Hollmann, W. B. (2022). Generative vs. usage-based approaches to language. In J. Culpeper, B. Malory, C. Nance, et al., eds., *Introducing Linguistics*. London: Routledge, pp. 449–458.

Holme, R. (2010). Construction grammars: Towards a pedagogical model. *AILA Review*, 23, 115–133.

Hudson, R. (2006). *Language Networks: The New Word Grammar*. Oxford: Oxford University Press.

Hunston, S. & Francis, G. (2000). *Pattern Grammar: A Corpus-Driven Approach to the Lexical Grammar of English*. Amsterdam: John Benjamins.

Hurford, J. R. (2012). *The Origins of Grammar: Language in the Light of Evolution*. Oxford: Oxford University Press.

Ivanova, A. A., Mineroff, Z., Zimmerer, V., et al. (2021). The language network is recruited but not required for nonverbal event semantics. *Neurobiology of Language*, 2(2), 176–201. http://doi.org/10.1162/nol_a_00030.

Jackendoff, R. (1977). *X-bar-Syntax: A Study of Phrase Structure*. Cambridge, MA: MIT Press.

Jackendoff, R. (2002). *Foundations of Language: Brain, Meaning, Grammar, Evolution*. Oxford: Oxford University Press.

Jackendoff, R. (2008). Construction after construction and its theoretical challenges. *Language*, 84(1), 8–28.

Jackendoff, R. (2010). *Meaning and the Lexicon: The Parallel Architecture 1975–2010*. New York: Oxford University Press.

Jackendoff, R. & Audring, J. (2019). *The Texture of the Lexicon: Relational Morphology in the Parallel Architecture*. Oxford: Oxford University Press.

Jackendoff, R. & Audring, J. (2020). Relational morphology: A cousin of Construction Grammar. *Frontiers in Psychology*, 11 (Article 2241). http://doi.org/10.3389/fpsyg.2020.02241.

Janda, L. J. (2007). From cognitive linguistics to cultural linguistics. *Word & Sense*, 8, 48–68. http://slovoasmysl.ff.cuni.cz/node/222.

Johnson, M. A. & Goldberg, A. E. (2012). Evidence for automatic accessing of constructional meaning: Jabberwocky sentences prime associated verbs. *Language and Cognitive Processes*, 28(10), 1439–1452.

Kelly, K. T. (1996). *The Logic of Reliable Inquiry*. Oxford: Oxford University Press.

Kuhn, T. (2012[1962]). *The Structure of Scientific Revolutions*, 50th anniversary ed. Chicago, IL: The University of Chicago Press.

Lakatos, I. (1970). Falsification and the methodology of scientific research programmes. In I. Lakatos & A. Musgrave, eds., *Criticism and the Growth of Knowledge*. London: Cambridge University Press, pp. 91–195.

Lakatos, I. (1974). The role of crucial experiments in science. *Studies in History and Philosophy of Science*, 4(4), 309–325.

Lakatos, I. (1978). *The Methodology of Scientific Research Programmes*. Vol. 1 of Philosophical Papers, edited by J. Worrall & G. Currie. Cambridge: Cambridge University Press.

Lakoff, G. (1987). *Women, Fire, and Dangerous Things: What Categories Reveal about the Mind*. Chicago, IL: The University of Chicago Press.

Langacker, R. W. (1987). *Foundations of Cognitive Grammar*. Vol. 1: Theoretical Prerequisites. Stanford, CA: Stanford University Press.

Langacker, R. W. (2002). *Concept, Image, and Symbol: The Cognitive Basis of Grammar*. 2nd ed. Berlin: Walter de Gruyter.

Langacker, R. W. (2005a). Construction grammars: Cognitive, radical, and less so. In F. J. Ruiz de Mendoza Ibáñez & M. Sandra Peña Cervel, eds., *Cognitive Linguistics: Internal Dynamics and Interdisciplinary Interaction*. Berlin: De Gruyter Mouton, pp. 101–159.

Langacker, R. W. (2005b). Integration, grammaticization, and constructional meaning. In M. Fried & H. C. Boas, eds., *Grammatical Constructions: Back to the Roots*. Amsterdam: John Benjamins, pp. 157–189.

Langacker, R. W. (2008). *Cognitive Grammar: A Basic Introduction*. Oxford: Oxford University Press.

Langacker, R. W. (2009). Cognitive (Construction) Grammar. *Cognitive Linguistics*, 20(1), 167–176. http://doi.org/10.1515/COGL.2009.010.

Laporte, S., Larsson, T., & Goulart, L. (2021). Testing the principle of no synonymy across levels of abstraction: A constructional account of subject extraposition. *Constructions and Frames*, 13(2), 230–262.

Leclercq, B. (2019). Coercion: A case of saturation. *Constructions and Frames*, 11(2), 270–289.

Leclercq, B. (2024). *Linguistic Knowledge and Language Use: Bridging Construction Grammar and Relevance Theory*. Cambridge: Cambridge University Press.

Leclercq, B. & Morin, C. (2023). No equivalence: A new principle of no synonymy. *Constructions*, 15(1). http://doi.org/10.24338/cons-535.

Legallois, D. (2022). *Une perspective constructionnelle et localiste de la transitivité*. London: Iste Group.

Levshina, N. & S. Moran. (2021). Efficiency in human languages: Corpus evidence for universal principles. *Linguistics Vanguard*, 7(s3). http://doi.org/10.1515/lingvan-2020-0081.

Lyngfelt, B., Borin, L., Forsberg, M., et al. (2012). Adding a Constructicon to the Swedish resource network of Språkbanken. In *Proceedings of KONVENS 2012 (LexSem 2012 workshop)*. Vienna, Austria: ÖGAI, pp. 452–461.

Lyngfelt, B., Borin, L., Ohara, K., & Torrent T. T., eds. (2018). *Constructicography: Construction Development across Languages*. Amsterdam: John Benjamins.

McCawley, J. D. (1982). *Thirty Million Theories of Grammar*. London: Croom Helm.

Meehl, Paul E. (1990). Appraising and amending theories: The strategy of Lakatosian defense and two principles that warrant it. *Psychological Inquiry*, 1(2), 108–141.

Montalbetti, M. (1984). After binding: On the interpretation of pronouns. Doctoral dissertation. Cambridge, MA: Massachusetts Institute of Technology.

Müller, S. (2018). *A Lexicalist Account of Argument Structure: Template-Based Phrasal LFG Approaches and a Lexical HPSG Alternative*. Berlin: Language Science Press.

Müller, S. (2023). *Grammatical Theory: From Transformational Grammar to Constraint-Based Approaches*, 5th revised ed. Berlin: Language Science Press.

Newmeyer, F. J. (1996). *Generative Linguistics: A Historical Perspective*. London: Routledge.

Newmeyer, F. J. (1998). *Language Form and Language Function*. Cambridge, MA: MIT Press.

Nikiforidou, K., Fried, M., Zima, E., & Bergs, A., eds. (to appear). *The Cambridge Handbook of Construction Grammar*. Cambridge: Cambridge University Press.

Noël, D. (2007). Diachronic construction grammar and grammaticalization theory. *Functions of Language*, 14(2), 177–202.

Noël, D. & Colleman, T. (2021). Diachronic Construction Grammar. In W. Xu & J. R. Taylor, eds., *The Routledge Handbook of Cognitive Linguistics*. New York: Routledge, pp. 661–674.

Nolan, B. & Diedrichsen, E., eds. (2013). *Linking Constructions into Functional Linguistics: The Role of Constructions in Grammar*. Amsterdam: John Benjamins.

Perek, F. (2012). Alternation-based generalizations are stored in the mental grammar: Evidence from a sorting task experiment. *Cognitive Linguistics*, 23(3), 601–635.

Perek, F. (2021). Construction Grammar in action: The English Constructicon project. *CogniTextes*, 21. http://doi.org/10.4000/cognitextes.2008.

Petré, P. & Van de Velde, F. (2018). The real-time dynamics of the individual and the community in grammaticalization. *Language*, 94(4), 867–901.

Popper, K. (1963). *Conjectures and Refutations: The Growth of Scientific Knowledge*. London: Routledge.

Popper, K. (1970). Normal science and its dangers. In I. Lakatos & A. Musgrave, eds., *Criticism and the Growth of Knowledge: Proceedings of the International Colloquium in the Philosophy of Science, London, 1965.* Cambridge: Cambridge University Press, 51–58. http://doi.org/10.1017/CBO9781139171434.007.

Popper, K. (2002[1959[1935]]). *The Logic of Scientific Discovery* [translation by the author of *Logik der Forschung*]. Republished. London: Routledge Classics.

Pullum, G. K. & Scholz, B. (2002). Empirical assessment of stimulus poverty arguments. *Linguistic Review*, 19(1–2), 9–50.

Pulvermüller, F., Cappelle, B., & Shtyrov, Y. (2013). Brain basis of meaning, words, constructions, and grammar. In T. Hoffmann & G. Trousdale, eds., *The Oxford Handbook of Construction Grammar*. New York: Oxford University Press, pp. 397–416.

Riesch, H. (2008). Scientists' views of the philosophy of science. Doctoral dissertation. London: University College London.

Sag, I. (2012). Sign-based Grammar: An informal synopsis. In H. C. Boas & I. A. Sag, eds., *Sign-Based Construction Grammar*. Stanford, CA: CSLI Publications, pp. 61–197.

Salkie, R. (1984). Review of *Thirty Million Theories of Grammar* by James D. McCawley. *Journal of Linguistics*, 20(1), 202–204.

Sampson, G. (1980). *Schools of Linguistics: Competition and Evolution*. London: Hutchinson.

Sampson, G. (2016). Rigid strings and flaky snowflakes. *Language and Cognition*, 8(4), 587–603.

Sandra, D. & Rice, S. (1995). Network analyses of prepositional meaning: Mirroring whose mind – the linguist's or the language user's? *Cognitive Linguistics*, 6(1), 89–130.

Scheel, A. M., Tiokhin, L., Isager, P. M., & Lakens, D. (2021). Why hypothesis testers should spend less time testing hypotheses. *Perspectives on Psychological Science*, 16(4), 744–755. http://doi.org/10.1177/1745691620966795.

Shirtz, S. & Goldberg, A. (forthcoming). The English phrase-as-lemma construction.

Smet, H., D'hoedt, F., Fonteyn, L., & Van Goethem, K. (2018). The changing functions of competing forms: Attraction and differentiation. *Cognitive Linguistics*, 29(2), 197–234.

Sommerer, L. & Smirnova, E., eds. (2020). *Nodes and Networks in Diachronic Construction Grammar*. Amsterdam: John Benjamins.

Sönning, L. & Werner, V. (2021). The replication crisis, scientific revolutions, and linguistics. *Linguistics*, 59(5), 1179–1206. http://doi.org/10.1515/ling-2019-0045.

Sprenger, J. & Hartmann, S. (2019). *Bayesian Philosophy of Science*. Oxford: Oxford University Press.

Tallman, A. J. R. (2021). Analysis and falsifiability in practice. *Theoretical Linguistics*, 47(1–2): 95–112.

Taylor, J. R. (2003). *Linguistic Categorization*, 3rd ed. Oxford: Oxford University Press.

Tomasello, M. (2003). *Constructing a Language: A Usage-Based Theory of Language Acquisition*. Cambridge, MA: Harvard University Press.

Tomasello, M. (2006). Construction grammar for kids. *Constructions* SV1–SV11, 1–23.

Tomasello, M. (2009). Universal grammar is dead. *Behavioral and Brain Sciences*, 32(5): 470–471.

Tomasello, M., Carpenter, M., Call, J., Behne, T., and Moll, H. (2005). Understanding and sharing intentions: The origins of cultural cognition. *Behavioral and Brain Sciences*, 28(5), 675–691.

Torrent, T. T. (2012). Usage-based models in linguistics: An interview with Joan Bybee. *Revista Linguíftica*, 8(1). https://revistas.ufrj.br/index.php/rl/article/view/4469/3241.

Traugott, E. C. (2022). *Ten Lectures on a Diachronic Constructionalist Approach to Discourse Structuring Markers*. Leiden: Brill Online.

Traugott, E. C. & Trousdale, G. (2013). *Constructionalization and Constructional Changes*. Oxford: Oxford University Press.

Uhrig, P. (2015). Why the principle of no synonymy is overrated. *Zeitschrift für Anglistik und Amerikanistik*, 63(3), 323–337.

Ungerer, F. & Schmid, H.-J. 2006. *An Introduction to Cognitive Linguistics*, 2nd ed. London: Pearson Education.

Ungerer, T. (to appear). Vertical and horizontal links in constructional networks: Two sides of the same coin? *Constructions and Frames*. https://tungerer.github.io/files/Ungerer-forthc-Vertical-and-horizontal-links.pdf (prepublished version).

Ungerer, T. & Hartmann, S. (2023). *Constructionist Approaches: Past, Present, Future*. Cambridge: Cambridge University Press.

Van de Velde, F. (2014). Degeneracy: The maintenance of constructional networks. In R. Boogaart, T. Colleman, & G. Rutten, eds., *Extending the Scope of Construction Grammar*. Berlin: Walter De Gruyter, pp. 141–179.

Van Valin, R. D., Jr. & LaPolla, R. (1997). *Syntax: Structure, Meaning and Function*. Cambridge: Cambridge University Press.

Wible, D. & Taso, N. (2010). StringNet as a computational resource for discovering and investigating linguistic constructions. In M. Sahlgren & O. Knutsson, eds., *Proceedings of the Workshop on Extracting and Using*

*Constructions in Computational Linguistics*. Stroudsburg, PA: Association for Computational Linguistics, pp. 25–31.

Wilkinson, M. (2013). Testing the null hypothesis: The forgotten legacy of Karl Popper? *Journal of Sports Sciences*, 31(9), 919–920. http://doi.org/10.1080/02640414.2012.753636.

Williamson, J. (2017). *Lectures on Inductive Logic*. Oxford: Oxford University Press.

Woschitz, J. (2020). Scientific realism and linguistics: Two stories of scientific progress. In R. M. Nefdt, C. Klippe, & B. Karstens, eds., *The Philosophy and Science of Language: Interdisciplinary Perspectives*. Cham: Palgrave Macmillan, pp. 143–177.

Xu, W. & Taylor, J. R. (2021). *The Routledge Handbook of Cognitive Linguistics*. New York: Routledge.

Yang, C. D. (2002). *Knowledge and Learning in Natural Language*. Oxford: Oxford University Press.

Ziegler, J., Bencini, G., Goldberg, A. E., & Snedeker, J. (2019). How abstract is syntax? Evidence from structural priming. *Cognition*, 193: 104045. http://doi.org/10.1016/j.cognition.2019.104045.

# Acknowledgments

Apart from bothering family members with my thoughts about this work, I have discussed some of them – thoughts, not family members – with colleagues, in particular with Ben Ambridge, Hans Boas, Ilse Depraetere, Evelina Fedorenko, Pâmela Fagundes Travassos, Francisco Gonzálvez-García, Dylan Glynn, Samantha Laporte, Benoît Leclercq, Dominique Legallois, Ben Lyngfelt, Jaakko Leino, Julian Pine, Naoaki Wada, and Alexander Ziem. I'm grateful for the insights they shared. Special thanks go to Benoît Leclercq for commenting frankly but constructively on an earlier version of this document as it was nearing its completion. Any inadequacies are mine only. I thank Alex Bergs and Thomas Hoffmann, the series editors, for having a little faith in me and for providing positive feedback. I'm also thankful for the comments by an anonymous referee, which helped me in sharpening the focus of this Element. I owe a special debt of gratitude to the University of Lille for giving me, by way of a sabbatical leave, the necessary time to think.

# Cambridge Elements ☰

# Construction Grammar

## Thomas Hoffmann

*Catholic University of Eichstätt-Ingolstadt*

Thomas Hoffmann is Full Professor and Chair of English Language and Linguistics at the Catholic University of Eichstätt-Ingolstadt as well as Furong Scholar Distinguished Chair Professor of Hunan Normal University. His main research interests are usage-based Construction Grammar, language variation and change and linguistic creativity. He has published widely in international journals such as *Cognitive Linguistics*, *English Language and Linguistics*, and *English World-Wide*. His monographs *Preposition Placement in English* (2011) and *English Comparative Correlatives: Diachronic and Synchronic Variation at the Lexicon-Syntax Interface* (2019) were both published by Cambridge University Press. His textbook on *Construction Grammar: The Structure of English* (2022) as well as an Element on *The Cognitive Foundation of Post-colonial Englishes: Construction Grammar as the Cognitive Theory for the Dynamic Model* (2021) have also both been published with Cambridge University Press. He is also co-editor (with Graeme Trousdale) of *The Oxford Handbook of Construction Grammar* (2013, Oxford University Press).

## Alexander Bergs

*Osnabrück University*

Alexander Bergs joined the Institute for English and American Studies at Osnabrück University, Germany, in 2006 when he became Full Professor and Chair of English Language and Linguistics. His research interests include, among others, language variation and change, constructional approaches to language, the role of context in language, the syntax/pragmatics interface, and cognitive poetics. His works include several authored and edited books (*Social Networks and Historical Sociolinguistics*, *Modern Scots*, *Contexts and Constructions*, *Constructions and Language Change*), a short textbook on *Synchronic English Linguistics*, one on *Understanding Language Change* (with Kate Burridge) and the two-volume *Handbook of English Historical Linguistics* (ed. with Laurel Brinton; now available as five-volume paperback) as well as more than fifty papers in high-profile international journals and edited volumes. Alexander Bergs has taught at the Universities of Düsseldorf, Bonn, Santiago de Compostela, Wisconsin-Milwaukee, Catania, Vigo, Thessaloniki, Athens, and Dalian and has organized numerous international workshops and conferences.

## About the Series

Construction Grammar is the leading cognitive theory of syntax. The present Elements series will survey its theoretical building blocks, show how Construction Grammar can capture various linguistic phenomena across a wide range of typologically different languages, and identify emerging frontier topics from a theoretical, empirical and applied perspective.

# Cambridge Elements ☰

## Construction Grammar

Printed in the United States
by Baker & Taylor Publisher Services